# Life Is A Spiritual Game

## A Handbook For Living

### bj King

Life is A Spiritual Game

bj King

Copyright © 2025 by bj King

Published by 1st World Publishing
P.O. Box 2211, Fairfield, Iowa 52556
tel: 641-209-5000 • fax: 866-440-5234
web: www.1stworldpublishing.com

First Edition

ISBN Softcover: 978-1-4218-3587-7

LCCN: Library of Congress Cataloging-in-Publication Data

All rights reserved. No part of this book may be reproduced or utilized in any form or by any means, electronic or mechanical, including photocopying or recording, or by any information storage and retrieval system, without permission in writing from the author.

This material has been written and published for educational purposes to enhance one's well-being. In regard to health issues, the information is not intended as a substitute for appropriate care and advice from health professionals, nor does it equate to the assumption of medical or any other form of liability on the part of the publisher or author. The publisher and author shall have neither liability nor responsibility to any person or entity with respect to loss, damages, or injury claimed to be caused directly or indirectly by any information in this book.

# Table of Contents

## Book One – Life Is A Spiritual Game

1. bj's Note to Readers . . . . . . . . . . . . . . . . . . . . . . . . . . . . . . . . . . . . . . . . 7
2. Preface . . . . . . . . . . . . . . . . . . . . . . . . . . . . . . . . . . . . . . . . . . . . . . . . . . . . 9
3. RULE # 1 – The game of life is a game of boomerangs . . . . . . . . . . . . . . .13
4. RULE # 2 – What you can imagine can happen . . . . . . . . . . . . . . . . . . . . 14
5. RULE # 3 – Your mind has three departments: Sub-conscious, Conscious and Superconscious . . . . . . . . . . . . . . . . . . .15
6. RULE # 4 – There is a Divine Plan . . . . . . . . . . . . . . . . . . . . . . . . . . . . . 17
7. RULE # 5 – Know thyself . . . . . . . . . . . . . . . . . . . . . . . . . . . . . . . . . . . . .18
8. RULE # 6 – The only thing stopping you is doubt, fear and imagining . . . . . . . . . . . . . . . . . . . . . . . . . . . . . . . . . . . . . . . . . . . 19
9. RULE # 7 – Ask and it shall be given unto you . . . . . . . . . . . . . . . . . . . . 20
10. RULE # 8 – You must control yourself . . . . . . . . . . . . . . . . . . . . . . . . . . . 22
11. RULE # 9 – Help is available; however, you must ask for it . . . . . . . . . 23
12. RULE #10 – Power of the spoken word . . . . . . . . . . . . . . . . . . . . . . . . . . 24
13. RULE #11 – All our enemies are within us . . . . . . . . . . . . . . . . . . . . . . . .26
14. RULE #12 – What we resist, persists . . . . . . . . . . . . . . . . . . . . . . . . . . . . 27
15. RULE #13 – There is only the now . . . . . . . . . . . . . . . . . . . . . . . . . . . . . .28
16. RULE #14 – Infinite Intelligence is the true Source . . . . . . . . . . . . . . . . .29
17. RULE #15 – Grace and Forgiveness transcend Karma . . . . . . . . . . . . . . .31
18. RULE #16 – Resentment will be "re-sent" to you . . . . . . . . . . . . . . . . . . 32
19. RULE #17 – Love is Infinite Intelligence in manifestation . . . . . . . . . . . 34
20. RULE #18 – The importance of gratitude . . . . . . . . . . . . . . . . . . . . . . . . 35
21. RULE #19 – Money is Energy . . . . . . . . . . . . . . . . . . . . . . . . . . . . . . . . . . 36
22. RULE #20 – The Universe is based on order . . . . . . . . . . . . . . . . . . . . . . 37

The Beatitudes

23. "Blessed are the poor in spirit: for theirs is the kingdom of heaven" 38
24. "Blessed are they that mourn: for they shall be comforted." . . . . . . . . 39

25. "Blessed are the meek: for they shall inherit the Earth.".............40
26. "Blessed are those who hunger and thirst after righteousness sake: for they shall be filled."...................41
27. "Blessed are the merciful: for they shall receive mercy."............42
28. "Blessed are the pure in heart: for they shall see God."..............43
29. "Blessed are the peacemakers: for they shall be called the children of God."..................................44
30. "Blessed are they which are persecuted for righteousness' sake: for theirs is the kingdom of heaven."...............46
   The Lord's Prayer ...................................................48

## Book Two – Mind to Mind Healing

1. Mind to Mind Healing, Dr. Byron Gentry .......................53
2. Amazing Secrets of Psychic Healing, Benjamin O. Bibb, D.D., His Methods........................................................61
3. Sound Healing..................................................77
4. How I Learned About the Silva Method......................83
5. Resonance and Intuition......................................93
6. Transcending Being Empathic...............................101
7. Prayer of Exorcism............................................112

## Book Three – The Oversoul and Reincarnation

1. Multi-Dimensionality and the Oversoul.....................115
2. Consciously Opening to the Oversoul .....................122
3. Meditation for Meeting Members of Your Oversoul......132
4. Rainbow Bridge to the Oversoul............................134
5. The Oversoul and Channeling..............................139
6. What Reincarnation is and How it Works ................150
7. History of Reincarnation....................................158
8. Reincarnation from a Personal Perspective..............166
9. Soul Retrieval, Mending the Fragmented Self...........171
10. Walk-ins, Walk-outs, Soul Transfers, Soul Braiding, Soul Merging and Composites.............................176

# Book One

# Life Is A Spiritual Game

# bj's Note to Readers

The Master Jesus approached me in meditation in February 1990 and suggested that He had a desire to write about what He really meant in the Beatitudes. I was very hesitant and did not take down the information He offered. I did not feel confident and I did not want to write anything that might fly in the face of current Christian beliefs. When He approached me again in December 2004, He made the suggestion again. After twenty years of following spiritual guidance, I felt more confident and I was personally curious as to what He wanted to say to Humanity today. I agreed to sit for the necessary dialogs with Him to receive the information in this book.

The next morning when I sat in meditation, I expected Him to start with the Beatitudes. Instead He began to speak of the Laws of Life, Universal Laws and how God has always intended that Human life on Earth is to be a game between God and Humanity. He spoke of God deliberately hiding within the Human heart and that the ultimate game of life would be "hide and seek." He stated that Humans would seek God everywhere outside themselves, but that eventually a few would awaken from amnesia and remember the energy that caused their heart to beat is the energy of God. They would look within their own hearts and find their connection to God. Then they would become co-creators with God to recreate Heaven on Earth. Through their heart connection to God, they would remember their connection to the Universe. They would remember the game and begin to remember the rules – the Laws of the Universe. He said it was time for these rules of life to be written down and that, in my soul contract, that I had agreed to be the scribe who would put them on paper.

He gave me the insights and asked that I write many of them as if they were my opinions or observations. I would have been more comfortable just quoting our actual dialogues, but that was not His preference.

Many people have asked me, "Do you actually see Him when He comes to you to have these conversations?" I have to answer yes and no. I first feel His Presence, then I begin to hear words that I recognize as not coming from my own thoughts, because they appear on the right side of my brain rather than on the left side where my normal thinking pattern appears. The syntax of His speech is still often a bit "biblical" to me. When we later did get around to His explaining His definitions of The Beatitudes, He was more precise in defining His definitions of the words as He meant them. When He moved on to the Universal Laws, His language became less biblical and more modern. Often, He would send me to the bookshelves to get a book He had already inspired someone else to write and ask me to read certain parts. I have listed those books as references and would encourage you to read them.

I write the dialogues on notebook paper during the meditations. When I write words that are my thoughts the words appear on the lines of the paper. When the words begin to be His inspired words my writing becomes perfectly spaced between the lines, rather than being on the lines. I do have an image of Him in my consciousness, but it is not clear enough that I could draw it because there is so much Light and energy that the image is indistinct.

He inspired *LIFE IS A SPIRITUAL GAME*, which seemed to be a separate book; then during later meditations, He spoke of The Beatitudes, The Lord's Prayer and the Universal Laws. Eventually, He asked that all this material be presented as one book.

Sometimes a seemingly insignificant incident may be a turning point in our lives. It is my hope that receiving this book is that kind of incident for you. Bless you.

**bj King – November 2004 Oklahoma City, OK**

# Preface

Life is a spiritual game. There are Laws that govern the game. We live on a planet, which is located in a galaxy, which is located in a Universe, which is located within an Omniverse (a collective of twelve Universes). Each Universe has Laws which govern that Universe. Pretending these Laws do not exist or being ignorant of these Laws does not cause these Laws to disappear nor does it cause them to cease to function. These Laws are called Universal Laws. I shall refer to them as the "rules of the game." If we attempted to play a game, and if we and the other players did not understand the rules of the game, we would experience confusion, depression, anxiety, mixed results and feelings of being out-of-control.

Currently fear, worry and doubt are the three strongest thought forms on the planet. During every television program, we watch we see ads for anti-depressants, anti-anxiety drugs, and antacids. To promote the sale of these items, the advertisers are invested in creating more fear, worry and doubt in the consumer. I believe Humanity's confusion, anxiety and depression are a result of our not understanding the rules of the game we are attempting to play.

The truth is that we are all unlimited beings and the only thing that holds us back is our individual beliefs, which have become collective beliefs. Thoughts that we accept as being true become our beliefs. The accumulation of all of our individual beliefs becomes our belief system. What we have been told and taught about Humans and the World are, for the most part, not true. We suffer from misinformation. We suffer from collective amnesia of who we really are and where we are from.

Every one of our thoughts is a thread in the fabric of what we experience as our life. Each one of us weaves the fabric of our own lives.

When more than one person agrees on something, it becomes a shared belief. The various social, spiritual, financial and political structures around the World are examples of shared belief systems. The combined individual thoughts and the beliefs we hold collectively weave the tapestry of Human consciousness, the results of which we are all currently experiencing. Each individual has the right to his or her own experience and, consequently, his or her own beliefs. We are always dealing with our own perceptions. Everyone has his or her own truth.

Each of us creates our own unique perspective of the World and Humanity based on our beliefs. Because of the Law of Freewill we do not have the right to infringe our beliefs on others. Needing to convince someone else about your truth implies that you doubt your own belief. We can only change the collective beliefs by changing our own individual thought forms and beliefs.

Quantum physicist, Michael Talbot points out in *THE HOLOGRAPHIC UNIVERSE* that physicists are now coming to the understanding that our reality is actually a reality of "possibility" and that Human thought affects particles and waves of Light. When physicists attempt an experiment with molecules of Light (the basic element of our Universe), they have discovered that the thought forms of the scientists who are performing the experiment affect the outcome of the experiment.

Thoughts and beliefs affect Light and, therefore, are the basis of all creation. Our thoughts create our beliefs. Each of us has a unique energetic signature derived from our thoughts and beliefs. The thoughts and beliefs we hold and express are projected into the Universe as energy vibrations. Each thought exists as a minute wave of energy called a thought form. By Universal Law, the mission of each thought form is to fulfill the intent of the thought – to carry out the thinker's desires or intentions. <u>Nothing and no one censors these thought forms except us</u>.

The Universal Laws of Magnetization and Attraction, being impersonal and uncensored, energetically match our thoughts and beliefs and reflect back to us events, circumstances, and relationships that match our thoughts and beliefs. Once a thought form, a core belief, is established within a person, incidents will occur to continue to provide evidence to the believer that the belief is true. At the conscious level we may profess that we love ourselves and that we do desire friendships and partnerships that are based on love, respect and caring. But if, in our sub-conscious, we do not believe we are lovable, or deserve love, we will continue to attract people into our lives who will mistreat and/or abandon us.

You first have a thought, the thought creates a belief and what you believe is what you experience - thought precedes belief, and belief precedes experience. These beliefs may be either conscious or sub-conscious. If the beliefs are sub-conscious, we may have no sense of responsibility for having accepted them as beliefs. We may consciously just believe, "That's just the way life is." Our sub-conscious beliefs are opaque to us, but will be apparent to others.

Our feelings are generated by our thoughts. First we have a thought, which generates a belief, which causes a feeling, and then we have a choice of action, reaction, non-action or non-reaction.

Thought forms are real, just as surely as radio waves, television waves, microwaves, and x-rays are real. We are not as aware of them because their energy vibration, or frequency, is outside the range of our Human senses. Our senses are limited to a specific range of frequencies. If we become much attuned to another person we can sometimes perceive what they are thinking. This is called telepathy.

Once we realize it is our thoughts and beliefs that determine what we experience, because it is "The Law," we can learn "The Law," and live within "The Law" by developing mastery over our thoughts and, therefore, develop different beliefs about the World and ourselves, and have the life we desire. This game is a process, not a one-time event. We did not get where we are overnight; our life will not change overnight. It can gradually improve. We must first look at what we think, examine our beliefs, decide which ones we wish to continue to have and replace the ones we wish to let go of with the ones we now wish to hold.

We all have self-concepts, your beliefs about how you see yourself, what you believe about yourself and your abilities. Some of these come from conditioning or programming. You can change them at any time. No one can accept or choose a belief except the believer.

We were given Freewill. We always have choice, although it may not always seem as if we do, because we are afraid of the consequences. The consequence of not personally making the choice is a life lived by default. We can make the choice to have a life by default, by not examining what we are thinking and, therefore, we remain ignorant of our core beliefs. Or we can have a life based on examining what we are thinking that causes these beliefs, which cause our feelings, which cause our reality. We can change our reality by changing what we are thinking.

The Master Jesus repeated this thought often:

**"CHANGE YOUR THINKING – CHANGE YOUR LIFE."**

If we don't realize we are playing a game and learn the rules, we will keep getting the same experiences even with different players. Each time we play the game, ignorant of the rules, we experience more struggle and the cost to us is higher. To keep thinking the same way, believing the same things, doing the same things and expecting different results is a form of insanity. I believe Humanity and, therefore, the World, is suffering from this form of Human insanity.

What follows are the rules as He gave us.

# RULE # 1 – The game of life is a game of boomerangs.

What you sow, so shall you reap.

Thoughts are things; what you think is what you get.

What you send out in word or deed returns to you.

If you give hate, you will receive hate.

If you give love, you will receive love.

If you give criticism, you will receive criticism.

If you give kindness, you will receive kindness.

If you give judgment, you will receive judgment.

If you give joy, you will receive joy.

If you cheat, you will be cheated.

If you trust, others will trust you. If you lie, others will lie to you.

If you give encouragement, you will be encouraged.

**Suggested affirmations:**

*I am a perfect idea in the Mind of Infinite Intelligence. I am expressing perfection.*

*My greatest expectations come to pass in miraculous ways.*

*What is rightfully mine comes to me immediately through Divine grace.*

# RULE #2 – What you can imagine can happen.

To play the game of life successfully, you must learn to imagine only the result you truly desire.

Worry that you will become diseased – and you will.

Visualize and imagine yourself being healthy – and you will be.

Imagine disaster – and you will experience disaster.

Imagine you are safe – and you will be safe.

Imagine loss - and you will lose.

Imagine winning – and you will win.

Imagine poverty – and you will experience poverty.

Imagine wealth – and it will be yours.

Make believe a life – either positively or negatively – and that is what you will experience.

**Suggested affirmations:**

I am healthy, wealthy and wise.

I live in a peaceful and benevolent Universe.

I am grateful all of my true heart's desires are manifested immediately through divine right action.

# RULE #3 – Your mind has three departments: Sub-conscious, Conscious and Superconscious.

The conscious mind sees life, as it "appears" to be, with disease, disaster, death, sickness, poverty, lack and limitation.

If you don't control your sub-conscious mind, the media or someone else will.

The conscious mind impresses the sub-conscious mind with its thoughts and emotions.

The sub-conscious mind, without judgment, carries out literally the "orders" of the conscious mind.

The sub-conscious mind has no sense of humor; you can joke yourself into an unhappy or disastrous experience. "I feel like I've been run over by a truck."

The sub-conscious mind is impressed by "make-believe" and "active faith."

The Super Conscious mind - is the God Mind or Divine Mind is filled with perfect ideas and solutions. It communicates with the conscious mind through intuition.

If we had perfect faith, we could make an affirmation once, but few of us have perfect faith. Continually affirming establishes the belief in the sub-conscious mind. We are not trying to convince or persuade God, but our own sub-conscious mind.

**Suggested affirmations:**

*I now accept the perfect job for me in the perfect way; I give perfect service and receive perfect pay.*

*If it is mine, I claim it. If it is not mine, I release my desire for it.*

*There are no lost opportunities in Divine Mind. I now accept the perfect relationship, job, home, office space, etc. for me. Every seeming obstacle is a stepping stone that leads me to perfection in all areas of my life.*

## RULE #4 – There is a Divine Design for your life.

You signed a contract with your soul before you entered the game for this round of play.

You suffer from amnesia regarding this contract until you choose to wake up.

You can recover your memory through paying attention to your intuition.

You came to fill a place no one else can fill.

There is something you are here to do, which no one else can do.

**Suggested affirmations:**

*I now accept the way for the Divine Design of my life to manifest. I allow the genius within me to now be released. I see clearly the perfect plan.*

*Reveal to me my perfect self-expression. Show me which of my talents to express.*

*I work with Spirit and follow the Divine Plan of my life.*

*The Divine Plan of my life now takes shape in definite, concrete experiences leading me to my true heart's desire.*

*New areas of divine activity now open for me and unexplained opportunities are presented.*

*I am free to express my true Self.*

# RULE # 5 – Know Thyself.

The goal of the game is joy, fulfillment, happiness and to fulfill your contract.

You must "know yourself" well enough to know what causes you to feel joy. You must know what makes you feel fulfilled, what makes you feel happy.

You must know your "true heart's desires," for these are the soul's desires for this life. You will fulfill your contract if you remember and allow yourself to be, do, have your true heart's desires.

Every desire uttered or expressed is a demand on the Universe.

**Suggested affirmations:**

*I am now willing to consciously know my true heart's desires.*

*I now know the beliefs I hold in my sub-conscious mind.*

*I now accept that I create the way I feel through my thoughts.*

*I am now willing to fulfill my unique role in the Divine Plan.*

# RULE # 6 – The only thing between you and reaching your goal, without struggle, is doubt, fear and imagining you won't reach your goal.

To win the game of life we must substitute faith for fear. Fear is misplaced faith – faith in a result we do not desire.

Fear is misdirected energy and must be redirected or transmuted into faith in the desired result.

Worry gives energy to create the undesired result.

**Suggested affirmations:**

*Every seeming obstacle in my path becomes a stepping stone taking me to my rightful place and my good.*

*There are no lost opportunities in the Divine Mind – what is for my highest good is now mine.*

*Everything happens for the best.*

# RULE # 7 – "Ask, and it shall be given to you, seek, and ye shall find, knock, and it shall be opened unto you." (Matthew 7:7)

Words and thoughts have tremendous vibratory effects.

Whatever we voice – we begin to attract.

Talk about what you desire – not about what you don't desire.

When we affirm truth – every untruth we hold in our sub-conscious surfaces to contradict it.

Often, just before a big achievement, demonstration or manifestation comes, we will experience what looks and feels like failure and discouragement. Don't give up. Perseverance and faith are always rewarded.

When everything seems to be going wrong – it is probably just the Universe rearranging itself to make a space for good in your life.

Hold your vision of the perfect result and give thanks for it.

Speak and act "as if" the life you are imagining has already manifested.

If you ask for success, but prepare for failure, you will get what you prepare for.

Impress your sub-conscious with expectancy. If you wish to move – pack your boxes. We must have "active faith."

What you seek is seeking you.

**Suggested affirmations:**

*What I seek is now seeking me.*

*I am grateful and give thanks for my perfect health.*

*I am always at the right place at the right time with all I need and desire.*

## RULE # 8 – You can't control any situation – unless you first control yourself.

You are the only person you can change. If you change – those around you will change.

If you become angry and lose control of yourself – your energy and power become misdirected.

Addiction displaces creative action and energy.

The only cure for addictions is redirection of intention, energy and action.

You and God constitute a majority.

**Suggested affirmations:**

*I now choose to express all my creative energy in a positive, life-affirming manner.*

*I accept my good and know that I am deserving of good. I choose to control my thoughts and feelings.*

# RULE # 9 – Help is available, but you must ask for it.

Because of the Law of Free Will, our soul, Angels and Infinite Intelligence are not allowed to intervene on our behalf unless we ask.

Ask someone who has your highest good in mind to hold the vision of a successful outcome with you.

**Suggested affirmations:**

*I now accept assistance from my soul and everyone I meet.*

*I am worthy to have help.*

*Others are willing and available to help me.*

# RULE # 10 – We are continually making laws for ourselves through our beliefs and spoken words.

I always win.

I always lose.

Bad things always happen to me.

Good things always happen to me.

I am never successful.

I am always successful.

I always find a close parking space.

I am always cheated out of my good.

I am never on time.

I am always on time. I am unlucky.

I am lucky.

Expectancy brings the expected result.

If you expect to be disappointed – you will be.

Watch your use of language and correct "idle words."

We manifest the sum total of our sub-conscious beliefs.

If we had perfect faith, we could make an affirmation once. Few of us have perfect faith. Continually affirming establishes the belief in the sub-conscious mind. We are not trying to convince or persuade God, but our own sub-conscious mind.

**Suggested affirmations:**

*I am a child of the Universe and deserve only good.*

*I accept perfect health, wealth and success.*

*I know I am capable of fulfilling my mission.*

*I know I am not alone.*

*I reach my goals quickly, easily and with great joy.*

# RULE #11 – All our enemies are reflections of what is within us.

If we send love and goodwill to anyone who speaks ill of us - or tries to harm us – the situation will resolve itself.

Bless your enemy and you rob him of his power over you or his power to harm you.

This is true of nations as well as individuals. Bless a nation; send love and goodwill to every person there. See them as having all they need and desire and they will have no need to attempt to harm you.

No person is just your enemy.

No person is just your friend.

Every person is your teacher.

**Suggested affirmations:**

*Every person I meet is a reflection of myself.*

*Every person I meet has a gift for me.*

*I, and every person I meet, is an expression of Infinite Intelligence.*

*Everyone I meet is a potential friend.*

# RULE # 12 – What we resist persists.

Inharmonious situations are reflections of lack of harmony within us.

If we give no emotional response to an inharmonious situation, it will fade away.

If we declare war against something, we give our energy to its continuing. Rather than being against anything, see what you desire instead.

**Suggested affirmations:**

*I accept peaceful coexistence of all life.*

*I accept safety for all dolphins and whales.*

*I see the oceans and streams clear and unpolluted.*

*I accept all people of the World living in peace, harmony and abundance.*

*I see all people of the World as free, joyful and addiction-free.*

*I see all people of the World fed, housed, clothed and healthy.*

*I see honest, caring, loving people holding political office. They have the highest good of the planet and Humanity as their priority.*

# RULE # 13 - The past and future do not exist – there is only the now.

Sorrow, regret, guilt and remorse tear down the cells of the body. Forgive yourself – forgive others. If the wrong cannot be righted, doing a kindness in the present can neutralize its effects.

Bless the past and forget it.

Bless the future and visualize it as you desire to live it.

Be totally in the now with all your consciousness present.

Look with wonder at that which is present – it is a gift.

**Suggested affirmations:**

*I forgive myself and anyone I perceive has ever harmed those I care about or me.*

*I know my future holds only good.*

*I am willing to be consciously present in the now at all times with all my gifts, senses and faculties.*

*I now release all my fears, guilt and grief, and see these thoughts neutralized by love.*

# RULE # 14 – Infinite Intelligence (God) is the only true Source of supply.

We cannot depend on our jobs, our spouses, our parents, our retirement fund, the stock market or social security as our source and feel secure.

We can lose our job, our spouses or our parents.

As we have seen, money markets and retirement funds can be mismanaged or stolen.

The stock market can crash.

Banks can fail; money can always be stolen, disappear or be devalued.

Knowing and depending on the true Source of supply is the only path of true security.

**Suggested affirmations:**

*I now draw from the Universal Substance that which is mine by Divine Right.*

*My wallet is filled with cash and my mailboxes are filled with negotiable checks made payable to me.*

*My good now flows to me in a steady, unbroken, ever-increasing stream of success, happiness and abundance.*

*Every person is a link in the golden chain of my good.*

*I am an irresistible magnet for all that belongs to me by Divine Right.*

*My supply is inexhaustible, immediate and endless and comes to me through grace in perfect ways.*

*I spend money and energy under direct inspiration wisely and fearlessly, knowing my supply is endless and immediate.*

## RULE # 15 – The Laws of Grace and Forgiveness transcend the Law of Karma.

Recognize a negative thought, cancel it - replace it with a positive thought.

Admit an error, ask forgiveness, and commit an act of love and generosity.

**Suggested affirmations:**

*I am karma free. I accept living under the Laws of Harmony, Grace, Balance and Love.*

*I forgive others and myself all past errors in judgment and action.*

# RULE # 16 – Resentment will be "re-sent" to you.

Resentment has ruined more homes than drink and killed more people than war.

If I resent someone else having wealth, I am saying I don't deserve wealth.

If I am envious of someone else's home or relationship, I am saying I don't deserve a nice home or a happy relationship.

If I resent someone else driving a beautiful car, while I drive an old car, I am saying I do not deserve to have a beautiful car.

If I resent someone for leaving me, or not loving me enough to stay with me, I will recreate the circumstances over and over in my life until I see myself as worthy of love.

**Suggested affirmations:**

*When you see what you would like to have that you perceive belongs to someone else, instead of resenting their good, say, "Through divine right action, I claim for myself a home, car, relationship, etc., equal to what I see."*

*I send out love and I receive love.*

*I send out joy and I receive joy.*

*I desire and accept wealth and health for everyone and myself.*

*I accept love and happiness for others and myself.*

*Divine Love within me now dissolves all fear, doubt, anger and resentment. Infinite Love flows through me and creates an irresistible magnet for my good to come to me under grace and in the perfect way.*

## RULE # 17 – Love is Infinite Intelligence (God) in manifestation, and the strongest magnetic force in the Universe.

When you send out real love - real love will be returned to you.

See only Infinite Intelligence (God) expressed in every living thing.

**Suggested affirmations:**

*Divine Love, through me, now dissolves all seeming obstacles and makes my way clear, easy and successful.*

*Divine Love within me now dissolves all fear, doubt, anger and resentment. Infinite Love flows through me and creates an irresistible magnet for my good to come to me.*

# RULE # 18 – Gratitude is important – and the first rule of abundance.

Be grateful for what you have – know you are powerful and you created the life you now have by your thoughts – know you can change it by changing your thoughts.

Be grateful for your problem – it gives you the gift of understanding your thoughts and how to correct them in order to have the result you desire.

We suffer loss through lack of appreciation.

Be grateful for your life – it is a gift.

**Suggested affirmations:**

*I am grateful for all I now have in my life.*

*I am grateful to be free and to live in a free country.*

*I am grateful to have Freewill choice.*

*I am grateful for my life.*

*I am grateful for the gift of this day.*

*I am grateful for the Earth and her great abundance.*

*I now give thanks that this property (or object) is sold to the right person or persons for the right price. The buyer and seller are perfectly satisfied. The transactions are accomplished with ease, grace, accuracy and honesty.*

# RULE # 19 – Money is energy – Infinite Intelligence is energy – Money is Infinite Intelligence in manifestation, as freedom from want and limitation, but it must always be kept in circulation and put to correct uses.

No person can attract money if they despise or fear it.

We must be in harmony with a thing to attract it.

If money is considered more important than people or love, it will bring disease, disaster and unhappiness.

Money is not the root of all evil – love of money, above all else, causes evil.

We limit our supply by limiting our vision.

**Suggested affirmations:**

*As my money goes out, immediately money comes to me through grace and in perfect ways.*

*Infinite Intelligence is the Source of my supply and every day is a good day.*

*My wallet is always filled with cash and my mailboxes are filled with negotiable checks made payable to me.*

# RULE # 20 – The Universe is orderly.

There are Universal Laws that keep the Universe operating in an orderly fashion.

Planets do not collide.

Space holds stars, planets and molecules apart. Infinite Intelligence, through the Laws of Gravity, Magnetism and Attraction, causes them to rotate around each other in an orderly fashion.

**Suggested affirmations:**

*I now accept Divine order established in my mind, body and affairs. My good comes to me now through grace and magical ways.*

*Rhythm, harmony and balance are now established in my mind, body and affairs.*

# The Beatitudes

A Prose Poem in Eight Verses from The Bible, Book of Matthew, Chapter V.

A Summary of the Essence of Jesus' Teachings as Explained to Me by Jesus in Today's vocabulary.

Through bj King - January 21, 2005

The *Bible* was written in the language and period of almost 2,000 years ago. Many different people wrote it. Translations from Aramaic and other languages to English can be unclear, because a certain word then could have many definitions, especially in Aramaic. Also, the number of times the *Bible* has been revised and translated tends to have distorted the original meaning of Jesus' message.

*Jesus concerned himself with teaching general principles, which always had to do with mental states. As a person thinks so they will become.*


**Matthew 5:3 from the King James Version:**

"Blessed are the poor in Spirit: for theirs is the kingdom of heaven."

**Matthew 5:3 from the Living Bible Version:**

"Humble Humans are very fortunate, for the Kingdom of Heaven is given to them."

**Matthew 5:3 from the Revised Standard Version:**

"Blessed are the poor in Spirit, for theirs is the kingdom of heaven."

**Matthew 5:3 from the New English Bible version:**

"How blest are those who know their need of God; the kingdom of Heaven is theirs."

**Matthew 5:3 from the Phillips Modern English Version:**

"How happy are those who know their need for God, for the kingdom of Heaven is theirs!"

**Matthew 5:3 from the Jerusalem Bible:**

"How happy are the poor in Spirit; theirs is the kingdom of heaven."

The word "poor" could mean impoverished, depleted, lacking in ability, absent of quality, low in potential, or deficient. It can also mean "simple." Jesus says His reference was to "simplicity." He was encouraging the people to refrain from complex rituals and creating spiritual hierarchies. He taught there is only one Spirit and that Spirit is within us and within all things. Connecting to that Spirit is a simple process and does not require structure, permission, intermediaries, prerequisites or process. It requires silence, intention, acceptance, Love and simplicity.

**Matthew from 5:4 the King James Version:**

"Blessed are they that mourn: for they shall be comforted."

**Matthew 5:4 from the Living Bible:**

"Those who mourn are fortunate! for they shall be comforted."

**Matthew 5:4 from the Revised Standard Version:**

"Blessed are they that mourn, for they shall be comforted."

**Matthew 5:4 from the New English Bible:**

"How blest are the sorrowful; they shall find consolation."

**Matthew 5:4 from the Phillips Modern English Version:**

"How happy are those who know what sorrow means, for they will be given courage and comfort!"

**Matthew 5:4 from the Jerusalem Bible:**

"Happy are those who mourn: they shall be comforted."

In Aramaic, "mourning" could mean sorrow, grief, pain, or regret.

Jesus says we always have the choice of learning by spiritual unfoldment or by painful experience. Most people do not seek God whole-heartedly unless trouble, sorrow or failure appears in their lives. <u>He says He was referring to the "value of mourning" as in "the act of purging and releasing."</u> When a person first experiences loss, whether this is through the death of a loved one, the death of a marriage, loss of health, loss of a career or job, loss of home, or loss of financial or social position, the first reaction is shock, depression and/or grief. When the shock passes and a person accepts the circumstance and releases what has been, they open a space for the new that can come. Grieving is clinging to – mourning is letting go, releasing, purging, which allows the emergence, the comfort of a new stage of life. Often, in retrospect, we can see loss was a blessing in disguise.

**Matthew 5:5 from the King James Version:**

"Blessed are the meek, for they shall inherit the Earth."

**Matthew 5:5 from the Living Bible:**

"The meek and the lowly are fortunate for the whole wide World belongs to them."

**Matthew 5:5 from the Revised Standard Version:**

"Blessed are the meek, for they shall inherit the Earth."

**Matthew 5:5 from the New English Bible:**

"How blest are those of gentle spirit; they shall have the Earth for their possession."

**Matthew 5:5 from the Phillips Modern English Version:**

"Happy are those who claim nothing, for the whole Earth will belong to them!"

**Matthew 5:5 from the Jerusalem Bible:**

"Happy the gentle, they shall have the Earth for their heritage."

In Aramaic the world "meek" could mean humble, poor, subservient, lacking self-respect, or self-effacing. None of these are the meaning Jesus intended in using the word. His meaning was "moderation, equilibrium, balance." In balance there is wholeness, fulfillment and blessing. There is no need to hoard. If hoarding ceased, there would be plenty of all for all. He reminds us that we never truly own anything; we are only stewards. We are most happy and fulfilled when we are steward-shipping only what we truly love. "Meek" can also mean "open to the will of God," which is a mental attitude that draws prosperity to an individual.

The word "Earth" does not refer merely to the terrestrial globe of Earth. Earth in this context means "manifestation or abundance." Manifestation is the result of cause. Causation is mental. "Earth" means the whole of our outer experience. To "inherit the Earth" means to have dominion over our outer experience through thought.

If we live in balance, moderation, with lovingly-directed thoughts, we will manifest the life our heart desires, because we are open to the will of God for our lives. God's will for our lives is joy, love, abundance and perfect health.

**Matthew 5:6 from the King James Version:**

"Blessed are those who hunger and thirst after righteousness; for they shall be filled."

**Matthew 5:6 from the Living Bible:**

"Happy are those who long to be just and good, for they shall be completely satisfied."

**Matthew 5:6 from the Revised Standard Version:**

"Blessed are those who hunger and thirst for righteousness, for they shall be satisfied."

**Matthew 5:6 from the New English Bible:**

"How blest are those who hunger and thirst to see right prevail; they shall be satisfied."

**Matthew 5:6 from the Phillips Modern English Version:**

"Happy are those who are hungry and thirsty for true goodness, for they will be fully satisfied!"

**Matthew 5:6 from the Jerusalem Bible:**

"Happy are those who hunger and Thirst for what is right: they shall be satisfied."

Jesus says "righteousness" does not refer just to right conduct, but also to right thinking in all areas of your lives. Right thinking is the only thing that will produce desired results. Righteousness can also mean harmonious thoughts. If you seek to be in harmony with your thoughts, the results will be a harmonious, fulfilling life. To "hunger and thirst" refers to praying constantly for wisdom and guidance.

Righteousness means being right in your heart. Through the heart you feel the Presence of your Creator. The heart is a powerful magnet, which generates life energy and draws to you all you need and desire.

The basics for righteousness are: unity, love, life, respect, honesty, justice, and kindness.

Jesus said: "You came to Earth to live from your soul's level of understanding, and when this occurs you will be at peace with yourself and God, and Earth will be transformed. 'Blessed are they who thirst' means to thirst to become a full-time Light of the World, and all else will be added for you."

**Matthew 5:7 from the King James Version:**

"Blessed are the merciful for they shall receive mercy."

**Matthew 5:7 from the Living Bible:**

"Happy are the kind and merciful, for they shall be shown mercy."

**Matthew 5:7 from the Revised Standard Version:**

"Blessed are the merciful for they shall obtain mercy."

**Matthew 5:7 from the New English Bible:**

"How blest are those who show mercy; mercy shall be shown to them."

**Matthew 5:7 from the Phillips Modern English Version:**

"Happy are the merciful, for they will have mercy shown to them!"

**Matthew 5:7 from the Jerusalem Bible:**

"Happy the merciful: they shall have mercy shown them."

Jesus says if you extend mercy, you will receive mercy. What matters most is that you be merciful in your thinking. If you commit kind deeds out of fear or in order to receive rewards or the good opinion or favor of others, you are being hypocritical and your rewards will be as tainted as your motive.

**Matthew 5:8 from the King James Version:**

"Blessed are the pure in heart: for they shall see God."

**Matthew 5:8 from the Living Bible:**

"Happy are those whose hearts are pure, for they shall see God."

**Matthew 5:8 from the Revised Standard Version:**

"Blessed are the pure in heart, for they shall see God."

**Matthew 5:8 from the New English Bible:**

"How blest are those whose hearts are pure; they shall see God."

**Matthew 5:8 from the Phillips Modern English Version:**

"Happy are the utterly sincere, for they will see God!"

**Matthew 5:8 from the Jerusalem Bible:**

"Happy are the pure in heart: they shall see God."

Jesus says, "God has no physical form, other than as everything and everything around you and yourselves." He says to "see" in this sense means to receive spiritual perception, spiritual sight; the sight that causes you to actually see everything and everyone as an aspect of God. To "see" God is to understand the truth of unity, all as One. "Purity" is to understand God as the only real Cause, the only real Power. This might be reworded as: "Blessed are they who recognize God as the only real Cause and Presence, not just in theory but practically, in every thought and area of their lives."

The word "heart" in the Bible can also refer to the sub-conscious mind. Head knowledge is learned expression. Heart knowledge is that which you live and actualize. You are called to re-educate the sub-conscious by practicing the Presence of God at all times in all circumstances. To be "pure in heart" is to have "innocent perception," to recognize that everything was created in innocence.

**Matthew 5:9 from the King James Version:**

"Blessed are the peacemakers: for they shall be called the children of God."

**Matthew 5:9 from the Living Bible:**

"Happy are those who strive for peace – they shall be called the sons of God."

**Matthew 5:9 from the Revised Standard Version:**

"Blessed are the peacemakers, for they shall be called the sons of God."

**Matthew 5:9 from the New English Bible:**

"How blest are the peacemakers; God shall call them his sons."

**Matthew 5:9 from the Phillips Modern English Version:**

"Happy are those who make peace, for they will be known as the sons of God!"

**Matthew 5:9 from the Jerusalem Bible:**

"Happy are the peacemakers: they shall be called sons of God."

Jesus says, "To become 'peacemakers' is to recognize the Oneness of Spirit and to implement that recognition in your thoughts and actions, to rise above a dualistic approach to living. You normally see life as a conflict between polar opposites. It is your challenge to end dualistic thinking." In the word "peacemaker," Jesus is not referring to our being diplomats, negotiators, counselors or ministers, as in the settling of disputes. He is referring rather to seeking to perceive wholeness in all things, to end separation and duality.

You have been conditioned by the presence of what appears to be opposites: up/down, male/female, in/out, forward/backward, black/white, happy/sad, light/dark. You are called to rise above viewing life as a conflict between these seeming opposites.

Light and dark are not opposites, but represent variable conditions of exposure to light sources. Males and females both contain male and female hormones and attributes. Each seeming opposite is a percentage of the presence of the whole.

Jesus says, "You have thus far seen the process of creating energy as a result of polar-resistive, friction-generated process. You are to move to see the possibility of magnetism – the space between the seeming opposites as your source of energy. You have the potential to end conflict and to create what seems to be free energy. You often create problems or conflicts for yourselves so you can feel smart, intelligent, accomplished when you resolve them."

**Matthew 5:10 from the King James Version:**

"Blessed are they which are persecuted for righteousness' sake: for theirs is the kingdom of heaven."

**Matthew 5:10 from the Living Bible:**

"Happy are those who are persecuted for being good, for the kingdom of heaven is theirs."

**Matthew 5:10 from the Revised Standard Version:**

"Blessed are those who are persecuted for righteousness' sake, for theirs is the kingdom of heaven."

**Matthew 5:10 from the New English Bible:**

"How blest are those who have suffered persecution for the cause of right; the kingdom of Heaven is theirs."

**Matthew 5:10 from the Phillips Modern English Version:**

"Happy are those who have suffered persecution for the cause of goodness, for the kingdom of Heaven is theirs!"

**Mathew 5:10 from the Jerusalem Bible:**

"Happy are those who are persecuted in the cause of right: theirs is the kingdom of heaven."

In Aramaic "persecution" meant "suffering." In English it implies an "intentional harassment or punishment."

"For righteousness sake" refers to "for love's sake."

Jesus says, "When you reach a point where you can consciously 'be' the love that you are, know you are an aspect of God (Love), you are empowered to transcend suffering or illusions. Through love you have power over any situation, but to prove this to yourselves, to really 'know' it, you must set yourselves up to overcome adversity through the power of love."

God=Love. When you know and completely understand this truth, illusions, adversities and hardships will cease to exist in your lives.

There is no virtue in martyrdom. There is no virtue or advantage in being persecuted or annoyed by other people. This cannot happen unless there is something within you that still matches this energetically. You will be treated as you expect to be treated, but this expectation must be backed by truth. What you see and experience at any time is your own concept of reality. You create the potential for hindrance and persecution by what you hold in your thoughts, beliefs and subconscious. When you know, believe, accept and understand you are aspects of God (Love) and think, act and hold the vibration of that aspect of yourselves you live in the kingdom of heaven.

Jesus was not a martyr. He accepted the persecution of the Romans and gave back love and forgiveness. He chose His form of death to prove the possibility of ascension and to prove there is life after death of the physical body.

# The Lord's Prayer

Translated directly into English from the original Aramaic using a modern understanding of the ancient grammar.

O Cosmic Birther, from whom the breath of life comes, who fills all realms with sound, light and vibration.

Soften the ground of our being and carve out a space within us where your Presence can abide.

Fill us with your creativity so that we may be empowered to bear the fruit of your mission.

Let each of our actions bear fruit in accordance with your desire. Endow us with the wisdom to produce and share what each being needs to grow and flourish.

Untie the tangled threads of destiny that bind us, as we release others from the entanglement of past mistakes.

Do not let us be seduced by that which would divert us from our true purpose, but illuminate the opportunities of the present moment.

For you are the ground and the fruitful vision, the birth, power, and fulfillment, as all is gathered and made whole once again.

Amen.

# Recommended Other Books on These Subjects

THE GAME OF LIFE AND HOW TO PLAY IT and YOUR WORD IS YOUR WAND – Florence Scovel Shinn – DeVorse & Company, P. O. Box 550, Marina Del Rey, CA. 90294.

BEFORE YOU THINK ANOTHER THOUGHT – Bruce Doyle III - Rare Shares Limited, 5415 Lake Howell d. 3 293, Winter Park, FL 32792.

THE HOLOGRAPHIC UNIVERSE – Michael Talbot – Harper-Collins Publishers, 10 East 53rd St. New York, NY 10022.

A COURSE IN LIFE Joan Gattuso – Jeremy P. Tarcher/Putnam, 200 Madison Ave. New York, NY 10016, www. Penguinputnam.com

THE LIFE YOU WERE BORN TO LIVE by Alan Cohn from New World Library.

A COURSE IN LIFE by Joan Gatttuso from Jeremy P. Tarcher/Putnam.

YOUR HEART'S DESIRE by Sonia Choquette from Three Rivers Press.

THE PSYCHE AND PSYCHISM by Torkom Saraydarian from Aquarian Educational Group.

RAYS OF DAWN by Thurman Fleet from Concept Therapy Institute.

SIMPLE ABUNDANCE by Sarah Ban Breathnach from Warner Books.

# Book Two

# Mind-to-Mind Healing

1.

# Mind-to-Mind Healing

## Byron Gentry

In the mid 80's after taking The Silva Method and gaining contact with my soul through meditation, I met a chiropractor named Byron Gentry. Byron knew immediately the first time I went to him for an adjustment who I am at the level of my soul, so he never charged me for helping me to keep my body tuned up. We became friends and appreciated each other's talents, work and sense of humor. I attended a series of classes he offered in his methods of healing and use of the Mind. He had the most developed control of his Mind of anyone I have ever met. His body was a bit deformed from having polio. He found through practice and his soul's suggestion that he could use his body as a pendulum to check out a person's body or the compatibility between two thoughts, organs or actions.

Byron believed in miracles. He believed in God and agreed that many miracles are the direct result of prayer and Divine intervention, but he also believed that a miracle can happen as a result of applying a higher set of laws to a particular condition to produce a different result than was previously experienced. The Law of Mind is a higher Law than our Earth and Human physical Laws.

He had learned and taught that the Mind can create a precise treatment with a thought of 1,000,000 vibrations per second of Positive, Universal, and Counterclockwise Energy, which he vitalized with intense emotion. Authority can initiate a new condition (by increasing or decreasing the vibratory rate) in the area being treated. He also reminded us that when treating a person's brain, that it was important to remember that different areas of the brain govern and stimulate every function, organ, and gland of the body. He believed talents and emotional traits have their own areas of control in the brain. When treating a condition, he admonished us to treat the part of the brain which controls the area we were treating.

He told us that all living things have an etheric double, which is a vibrational image or pattern of the physical form, and that all experiences are registered in the etheric double.

He knew and taught that every person and object in the World has its own individual rate of vibration, including cities. Some vibratory frequencies are compatible and others are not. Even the tiniest microorganism, including diseases, has a vibratory rate. He taught me how to check with a person's soul to find out the true cause of their illness or the condition of their body, and to check the vitality of each organ of their body. He tested and asked Universal Mind for the optimal frequency of vibration for each organ of the Human body. He would first test the person's frequency of each organ and then mentally adjust the frequency with his Mind to the optimal frequency. The following are the numbers he was given by Universal Mind that he used to mentally adjust the frequency of his patient to their optimal vibration:

**Human Body organ frequencies he used:**
Brain frequency range 72-90 MHz
Normal Brain frequency 72 MHz
Genius Brain frequency 80-82 MHz
Normal Human Body 62-78 MHz
Human body: from neck up 77-78 MHz
Human body: from neck down 60-68 MHz
Thyroid and Parathyroid glands 62-68 MHz
Thymus gland 65-68 MHz
Musculoskeletal System: 40-45
Nerve Systems: 30-35
Heart 67-70 MHz
Lungs 58-65 MHz
Liver 55-60 MHz
Pancreas 60-80 MHz

**Some diseases:**
Disease starts at: 58 MHz
Colds and flu start at: 57-60 MHz
Candida overgrowth starts at: 55 MHz

Receptive to Epstein Barr at: 52 MHz
Receptive to Cancer at: 42 MHz
Death begins at: 25 MHz

After checking the organ's frequency, he would check to see if anything was blocking the flow of energy to that organ, and align it and raise the vibration of the organ with a mental command to bring it up to the optimal frequency.

He mentally increased the power of the mental healing he sent by focusing the thought form through a large quartz crystal and a large ruby crystal he created with his Mind. He would think the words crystal and ruby and say "energize, energize, energize" three times. He projected his mental thoughts using all three of his faculties: mental, physical and emotional. When he wasn't satisfied with the strength of his mental sending vibration, he mentally projected that each time he treated a patient, his own mental level would increase and the part of his brain that controlled his ability to do the mental projecting would progressively become stronger. Later, he mentally created a mental laser beam through which he projected his thoughts, sending the thought through the imaginary crystal, ruby and the mental laser beam after he had energized the thought three times with the word "energize."

He also learned and taught us to make a sound as we released and projected the mental thought into the Body and Mind of the person we were sending the message to by either snapping our fingers or clapping our hands. He used the motion of gripping his fists when making a sound was not convenient in any given situation. He admonished us that our decree needed to always be worded in a positive way and in present time because he knew that words themselves contain incredible power.

Two of the words he discovered that carry an enormous amount of power are "normalize" and "neutralize." He also used the words "return to an injury-free state" when addressing an organ that had been damaged or diseased. He learned that using these methods, he could address unknown parts of the brain which control such areas as hearing, sight, addiction, negative emotions and personality traits, to command that particular thought center to "normalize." He realized his treatments only worked if he launched them with emotion and physical action. Even though he knew many of his Ah Hah's came from Universal Mind, he attributed many of his discoveries to accidentally coming to the awareness of his methods.

He learned that the Human body is polarized and caused to vibrate in specific patterns because it exists within this tremendous flow of energy between the Earth's poles. Because Humans are electromagnetic Creatures, the Mind and Body are subject to the physical Laws of Magnetism. If the polarity is positive, good things, such as health, wealth and happiness are attracted to it. If it is charged negatively, the reverse is true and trauma on all levels results.

He discovered that not only is the individual body polarized, so are each of the body's organs and systems. He discovered once again that the magic word to effectively reverse polarity is "normalize." He taught that the proper alignment for a Human is with the head polarized to the North Pole and the feet to the South Pole. He discovered that when he projected the command to normalize the polarity of a patient, the polarity of the person's body reversed immediately with beneficial results. I wonder how this treatment would affect the body of a person who is diagnosed as bipolar? This subject was not addressed in his class.

Once Byron learned about polarity, he taught that we should treat each of the body parts individually and normalize the polarity of each organ. He believed that a diseased organ would never heal completely unless the polarity was normalized and brought back to its healthy vibratory rate. He achieved this with the word "normalize" and projected it mentally with emotion and a physical action.

Byron also taught us that we could call upon the Holy Spirit or the Universal Intelligence when we needed guidance in any situation. He also taught us that static electricity could occur at any point in the body and create mid-level to devastating results. Static electricity always occurs from the blockage of a nerve impulse. When a nerve impulse isn't allowed to complete its circuit from the nerve stimulus to the intended organ or system, static electricity builds up. The static electricity will remain at that point until the blockage is removed. If the blockage is not removed, damage to the organs of the system often results.

He taught that many things can block a nerve impulse, either totally or partially. The most common blockage results from misaligned vertebrae. He always realigned the patient's spine after doing his mental treatments. Static electricity can also build up in the heart, for example, as a result of blocked impulses. If untreated, this condition can accelerate until the heart goes into spasm generating up to 190 units of static electricity, which is usually fatal.

Byron told us his order of treatment usually started by first checking the overall energy level of the person, then checking each organ that he suspected was affected by static electricity. Then he normalized the polarity of the organ and its nerve supply mentally. This caused the organ to have an improved chance of recovery, and it could return to its normal condition. If the blockage resulting in build-up of static electricity were allowed to continue, the organ would almost certainly be damaged.

By dissipating a build-up of static electricity, a diseased organ is often able to complete the healing process and return to normal condition. Static electricity and reversed polarity greatly hinder the function of any organ, but especially one that is already impaired by a disease.

He taught us that every change in the environment experienced by a Human being over the course of an entire lifetime is registered in the synapses of the brain. When these synapses are impaired by a build-up of static electricity, the flow of normal energy is blocked and negative consequences can result.

By de-energizing and dissipating static electricity in the synapses of the brain, the normal, natural flow of energy is restored, and health and freedom from a variety of debilitating conditions results. Static electricity is a very real force, and can be a potentially deadly one because there is no known machine available with the ability to measure its presence other than to ask the body intelligence or soul of the patient. The only method available to Byron was to use his pendulum body to identify and calculate the presence of static electricity. He could de-energize and dissipate static electricity in the body he was treating without knowing how much was present or in the exact location. He used the word "dissipate" along with "neutralize" and "normalize" repeatedly in his treatments. When he used it, I noticed he always said it three times: "dissipate, dissipate, dissipate," the same way we use it to dissipate a storm. He told us that accurate and appropriate energized thought projection directed toward a suspected traumatized organ or system can be extremely effective in dealing with the debilitating force of static electricity.

After Byron dissipated the static electricity and corrected the polarity, he projected the normal organ vibration referenced by the previous list. He believed these three elements, polarity, static electricity and velocity, working together, created a tremendous healing environment. He also came to know and taught us that the velocity or speed of vibrations for an entire body should be 108,000 vibrations per second for optimum health and fitness, and made it a point to check whole-body velocity as part of his normal treatment procedure.

He learned and taught that the speed of vibrations entering an area or a body, when normal and healthy, the velocity would be 108,000 vibrations per second of counterclockwise energy. If a person's body was vibrating lower than 108,000 per second he would increase the velocity to 200,000 vibrations per second with his Mind. Dysfunction occurs when the vibrations enter a structure or a person in a clockwise manner and are increased in this negative vibratory direction.

Later in life he studied acupuncture. He learned there are 14 meridians in the body through which energy flows. If any of these become blocked, energy is not able to flow correctly. He began to do the treatment mentally by mentally inserting imagined needles in the pressure points for long distance healing and needles for his in-office patients.

His interest in polarity led him to consider the ley lines of the Earth and our mental ability to change them from negative to positive. One of his teachers, Ida Roff, taught him about ley lines. She told him that ley lines run from both the North and South Poles and converge at the equator. They encircle the globe in lines approximately ten feet apart from east to west. They are invisible to most people, but many psychics are able to see them. These powerful energy fields can be very destructive if misaligned, but if the polarity of the ley lines is normal, the effect created is harmonious. Since everyone lives within ley lines, the positivity or negativity of the ley lines is determined by the thoughts and emotions of the inhabitants. Often if a person moves into a home where there has been discord, they will not feel happy or secure in the home because the ley lines have become negative. The building up of negativity causes a blockage in the flow of energy through the house. I thought about areas where businesses seemed to fail no matter what kind of business or restaurant opened on that piece of land.

Byron spoke of the ley lines in the same way he had grasped acupuncture and mentally created spikes that he could mentally insert in a ley line he found to register as negative when he checked it with his body pendulum. He mentally normalized the polarity on both the north and south sides of the property to be treated. He used the word normalize, spoken with emotion accompanied by a physical action such as clapping his hands. He then mentally created a spike, imagining it to be an enlarged version of an acupuncture needle, mentally energized it, and with the power of his Mind, drove it into the ley lines both north and south of the area to be treated.

Byron taught us that the most incredible and powerful asset we have is our Mind and our ability to imagine. He reminded us that thoughts produced by our Minds are very real and that thoughts can harm as easily as they can heal. He believed that carefully directed positive thoughts can be as potent as medicine. With training and practice, he convinced us that it is possible to use our thoughts as precisely as a laser beam. He taught us that, when spoken and/or projected mentally and accompanied by intense emotion and a physical activity, such as snapping the fingers or clapping the hands, these commands produce incredible tangible results. Centered on three elements, polarity, static electricity, and velocity, these commands may be used to heal, comfort, reverse negative situations, and much more.

Byron taught us about time, that time is relative and that it can be mentally manipulated. He said five hours of energy can be mentally projected into an area or condition in five seconds and that treatment can be projected to occur at any time, or at set intervals, at a predetermined intensity. He taught that in the thought realm, there is no time or space. We, with our mental activity, are the determinant factor. All things are possible when we become masters of ourselves and our environment, which includes time and space.

Before such mastery is possible, it is necessary to become keenly aware of our thoughts and aware of everyday surroundings and the effects they have upon our Mind and body. He pointed out that very few people realize the profound effect even simple, ordinary things can have on their body, or that everything we perceive with our senses (sight, hearing, smell, touch and taste) can either strengthen or weaken us.

He taught us that many of his techniques appear simple, but some are not; that it would require a great deal of patience and practice before we could become truly proficient with them. He did ask us not to become discouraged by what he called the "learning curve," and to persevere and practice. He said the wonderful thing about applying any part of what he offered us, regardless of how small or inept it might be, would always accomplish some good, and at the same time, strengthen and increase our effectiveness. He admonished us to increase our personal power and awareness and that if we did, new ideas and insights would begin to appear.

During the five years I traveled away from Oklahoma City, I called him when I needed help and he could adjust my spine over the phone. If I felt ill in any way, before he treated me, he would ask me to drink a glass of water with two tablespoons of apple cider vinegar in it to correct the ph of my system.

While away from Oklahoma, I missed his humor, his wonderful personality and presence and having him physically present to help me with my body. When I returned to Oklahoma City, I was disappointed and devastated to learn that he had passed from his body and would not be there physically to help me with my body. Several years later, he began to communicate with me during meditation. He offered himself as a mentor and assistant to me and to various healers I read for. He is also available from where he is now to communicate with us and to help us to heal ourselves and others.

## 2.

# Amazing Secrets of Psychic Healing

## Benjamin O. Bibb, D.D.
## His Methods

In 1987, I was traveling from Oklahoma City, OK, to Portland, OR. A friend in Oklahoma City had convinced friends of hers in Portland to host me in their home for a few days during my travels. While I was there, they talked about a friend of theirs who did psychic healing using his Mind and imagination. They showed me a book he had written. I was amazed to see it was co-authored by Benjamin O. Bibb with Joseph J. Weed, the author who wrote the book *Psychic Energy* that had been thrown off the shelf at me in 1982. At that time, my soul was ready for me to have direct communication with my soul by meditating to receive inspired writing.

I studied Ben's methods during my stay in Portland and was very impressed by the stories of Ben's successes. Ben stressed that the Mind is the healing agent and pointed out that the Mind is not the brain. That The Mind uses the brain like a tool, but that the Mind is limited all too often by the brain's erroneous convictions as to what can be done and what cannot. The Human Mind is capable of doing many amazing things. Ben did not consider the methods he used and taught to be inspirational, religious or spiritual. He considered it to be a scientific way to remove the blocks to self-healing. Even though he did not consider it spiritual, he did state, "No work of Humans, great or small, can be accomplished without Divine Assistance, but some Human effort is required."

He taught that the first secret to being able to assist others and onesself with his methods was to learn how to contact our own sub-conscious Minds, and then the inner or sub-conscious Mind of the person to be healed. He taught that when you learn this, you will be able to "see" the subject mentally and to identify the illness, injury or other distress, including the parts of the body affected. This "in-picture" visualization can be triggered by expanding your imagination from an ordinary daydream condition. He did stress that a "sincere effort" on the part of the person desiring to learn to heal is required. Effort is required to learn to heal just as it is to learn any worthwhile objective in life.

It felt important to me that the same method of meditation I had been taught in the Silva Method to move into the Alpha brain wave frequency was the same one that Byron Gentry and Ben Bibb also used.

The important thing to accomplish (which we were able to do with the 3,3,3 then 2,2,2, then 1,1,1 and 10-to-1 method of counting and breathing to reach Alpha) is to close off our attention to the left brain chatter and to focus on the right brain through which we could contact our Sub-conscious and the Sub-conscious of the individual being treated.

Ben often stated in his lectures "The powerful Inner Mind, which created the physical body from a single cell and keeps it alive and functioning, can also heal any imperfection that may develop. It does not always recognize these malfunctions and occasionally is at a loss as to the best method of correcting them. It is in such situations that you, as the healer, can function most effectively by pointing out to the subject's Inner Mind just what is wrong and what should be done to correct it. Our service as Mind-to-Mind healers is not to replace or compete with doctors and medical practitioners, but to augment the work they do with energy and positive thought forms."

Ben conceived and developed the idea of a mental telephone to reach the Inner Mind of the person to be healed by using his imagination and concentration. First, we have to have a strong desire to make the Mind-to-Mind contact. If we do not focus just on the right side of our brain, our conscious thoughts will attempt to convince us that this will not work and is not possible. You do have to have a definite individual you desire to contact. It is helpful to have the name, age, sex and address or location of the actual person (not an imaginary one) that you intend to contact. This is also something we were taught in the Silva Method. It is important that the person has an ailment or injury and that we have the intention to do good or to help this person.

## THE MENTAL TELEPHONE METHOD

Sit where you will not be disturbed, take the three deep breaths doing the 3,2,1 breathing then count backward from 10 to 1 to relax your body and slow your brain frequency. When you are relaxed and calm, mentally pretend to pick up a telephone you've created with your imagination and mentally dial the number of the person you wish to reach, if you know the actual number. If you do not know the number of the person you wish to reach, dial any number with the appropriate number of digits (7 or 8 or 10). If you do not dial, then ask the operator to get you the party you wish to contact, giving the operator the name and location. When you feel you have made contact, mentally give your name and ask if the person wishes to be healed. Only if you receive an outright "no" do you disconnect. If you feel you have made the connection, ask the person to indicate the part of their physical body that requires attention by placing their hand on the area. Do not doubt the impressions you receive, whether it comes in words, a picture or knowingness. Accept what you receive as fact. Do not depend upon the way the problem has been diagnosed by hospitals or doctors. You can get direct firsthand information by looking at the person's body. Make sure you examine the entire body thoroughly and ask your Inner Mind to point out to you the area or areas where the cause of the problem lies. Remember it may take some practice before you feel you are making the connection. You must have a definite person in Mind that needs healing. Once you have done this you will intuitively know what needs to be done to help the healing. Forget yourself and focus on the person you wish to aid. Your purpose is to employ your Inner Mind to make contact with the Inner Mind of the subject to be healed. Good concentration is absolutely necessary. You learn by practicing.

Another possible way to connect after you relax and take the breaths is to allow yourself to drift mentally and imagine yourself standing next to the person who needs your help. Take time to observe the person and something of the surroundings. In this subtle way you can transport yourself from the imaginary to the real. With your etheric body, you can travel anywhere.

During the Silva Method training as well as in Ben's method, it is suggested that we make 3x5 cards, each with a different person's information that needs healing, and to use these cards to practice.

Do not be concerned that what you are doing is purely imaginary. There is no such state as "purely imaginary" in the sense that it exists only in the imagination of the thinker and nowhere else. The Human Mind is automatically creative, which means that every thought and every imagining held in the Mind has factual existence. The solidity of that factual (or material) existence depends upon the power of the creative thought and the force of the emotion behind it; thus, the greater your desire to make a successful Inner Mind contact, the more forceful will be your imagining. But don't get uptight or this will defeat your purpose. Stay calm and relaxed in a dream state so that your imaginary pictures will be sustained longer. The longer a clear thought is held the more it "solidifies" and the nearer it comes to materialization. When the same thought is repeated clearly at intervals, an enhanced and strengthened effect is produced. This is why at the end of a treatment, Ben always asks the person's Sub-conscious to repeat the treatment at intervals he describes.

Every Human being is comprised of three thinking entities. All three are "you," but each of these entities is distinct from the others and appears to function apart from the other two. These three thinking entities are:
1) The Conscious Mind which operates with words and logic
2) The inner or subjective Mind (the sub-conscious) which operates with pictures
3) The Higher Mind (sometimes referred to as the soul)

The Conscious Mind is the only one of which most people are ever aware. It is wholly dependent upon the brain, which is our contact with the physical World through the senses of sight, hearing, touch, taste and smell. These senses record the impressions they receive from outside physical stimuli and then send them on to the brain which records them and then translates them in turn to the conscious. These impressions are also permanently impressed upon the Inner Mind without the Conscious Mind being aware of it.

We are inclined to the perfectly natural mistake of assuming that the Conscious Mind is the only Mind and therefore the entire "self." It is not. There is no question but that it is in control of you, your life and most of your voluntary actions. Because the impacts on our five outer senses are so powerful and often so dramatic, we have a tendency to ignore our other senses, our other sources of information. We have other senses: a sense of balance, a sense of both physical and emotional exhaustion, a sense of muscular fatigue and so on. All of these senses send their information to the Sub-conscious Mind as well as to its conscious counterpart, but all too often the Conscious Mind ignores it. Another frailty of the Conscious

Mind is that it works entirely through the brain.

These limitations of the Conscious Mind are mentioned in order that you may better realize what an important part the Sub-conscious or Inner Mind plays in a Human's life. The Inner Mind has equal importance with the Conscious Mind and in many ways it is more powerful, so it is necessary for us to know about it and understand some of its functions.

The Inner Mind can do amazing things, any of them impossible from the viewpoint of the Conscious Mind. It constructed the Human body, your body, from a single cell. Compared to this, healing a wound or correcting a bodily malfunction is a relatively insignificant task. Your Inner Mind not only constructed your body, but keeps it functioning twenty-four hours a day. Can you imagine just trying to keep your heart beating via impulses from your Conscious Mind? We should not make the mistake of regarding our heartbeat as "automatic." It only appears that way to your Conscious Mind. All of our bodily functions, including breathing, digestion, elimination, etc., are intelligently and continuously directed, but since this activity is below the awareness level of the Conscious Mind, it dismisses the entire wonderful performance as "automatic," with little more than passing curiosity.

There is nothing wrong with this arrangement. In fact, this is the way it should be in order to give the Conscious Mind and its tool, the brain, a chance to develop. This development process still has a long way to go, as is indicated by the fact that we use, on the average, less than ten percent of our brain's capacity. When we ignore the Inner "I," we neglect a most powerful instrument which is there for us to use, if we but try. For one thing, we can use it to heal ourselves and to heal others.

When we came into being, our Inner Mind was programmed to create a certain type of body and to keep it functioning smoothly, or as smoothly as our Conscious Mind and our emotions would permit. The Inner Mind does not reason nor form judgments and make decisions, but usually accepts, without question, the attitudes adopted by our conscious nature. The Inner Mind can be reached, however, and it will usually follow constructive suggestions. It is this willingness to accept instruction that we employ in our healing work.

The Higher Mind, or soul, is where the "I," the real self, usually resides. This part of us is most powerful and, when called into action, can wield physical matter and events as easily as our hands can shape wet clay. In the present stage of the average Human's development, and this applies to most of us, it stands aloof so that the Conscious Mind, through trial and oft-repeated mistakes, may learn the true nature of energy and how to put it to the best use. In Ben's teaching, in his healing work, he taught students to only rarely approach the soul, which really surprised me. I personally mentally contact the soul and the "body intelligence" when I first connect with a person to be healed and find it makes me privy to information that would be difficult for me to discern from my inner vision. Ben may have considered connection to the person's Sub-conscious Mind is the same as the "body intelligence."

It is the Inner Mind or the Sub-conscious Mind that does the healing. It will also communicate with you, the healer, the exact nature and location of the injury or malfunction so that an accurate appraisal may be made.

The method most frequently used:

1. Go through the 3, 2, 1 and the 10-to-1 meditation process to relax your body and to take your brain to the Alpha level.
2. Contact the Inner Mind of the subject and observe the true nature of the injury or malfunction. When you have made the contact, ask the Inner Mind of the subject to become calm. Soothe their agitated nerves by imagining the person calm, then fill and surround them in an aura of Blue Light energy.
3. Use mental pictures to show the subject's Inner Mind how to correct this. Pictures convey the impression far more clearly than feelings or words. Words are particularly unreliable because they, too, are symbols and often mean different things to different people. A picture clearly shown is unmistakable.
4. Supply healing energy and instruct the subject's Inner Mind to repeat the process you have just accomplished on an ongoing basis for as long as the problem exists. (Ben always started with Golden Sun White Light energy and sometimes added Blue Light energy to calm pain, Green Light energy to calm nerves and to heal, and Pink Light energy when dealing with emotional issues or the heart.)
5. See the subject perfectly healed, then break contact gently and give no further thought at that time, although the treatment may be repeated by you at a later time.
6. Pain always has a cause; seek to find the source and cause of the pain.

**Ben created several mental substances that he used in his healing methods:**

Mental gold glue

Human putty

Human tape

Human putty bone builder and bone cement

Mental ice packs with Blue Light energy to reduce pain and swelling

Golden oil to lubricate joints or between vertebrae - a combination of olive oil and honey

Narrow strips of people rubber or elastic strips for attaching things into place and to strengthen or reinforce ligaments, cartilage and muscles

Porous tape for wrapping a corrected joint or opening

Shrinking paste to shrink swelling

Sea water to wash out the stomach, gall bladder, liver or other organs, asking the body to use only the nutrients the body needed from the water and eliminating what was not needed

Transparent healing tape to correct an eye problem

Never cut the skin, just pluck out a tumor or growth with your fingers

He used Turquoise Light energy to calm pain, which is a combination of Blue and Green energy

Golden sponges for soaking up liquid or pus

He created drains to drain the lungs or sinuses by siphoning the liquid away

Infected areas he washed with a germicide solution he mentally created

He considered allergies to be a false response of the autoimmune system to the essence of the substance causing the reaction

He created an auric flashlight that he used to better inspect the insides

He mentally used an emery board or sandpaper to file away calcium deposits on the joints

Bone cement to hold together broken bones

He consistently used the words "normalize," "energize," "dissipate" and "neutralize" when addressing the body or an organ. He always said the word three times.

He washed out the stomach and intestines with White Light energy when called for

He sealed blood vessels with cotton strips to stop bleeding and demanded the blood to coagulate

When dealing with gall stones, he collected and put them in a sack made of Human skin and left them in the gall bladder because removing them would cause an imbalance, containing them kept them from clogging the opening

Bicarbonate of soda Blue paste to cover rashes and skin inflammations

He demanded the body to raise its frequency and sometimes toned after the demand

He used the Blue Light energy of Protection

He always energized his food and any supplements with love before ingesting them

He recommended grounding into the magnet at the core of the Earth to strengthen the iron in a person's body

These techniques fully exemplify that "what you see is what you get." In less simple language, this means that whatever you clearly imagine for the person asking for help, that is the direction and form the help will take. So if our imagination is half-hearted or less than complete, the results will be proportionally diminished. Think positively; always be confident in the success of your efforts and they will be rewarded.

Healing is God's work; we are only the instruments, the channel through which God performs miracles of healing. When using the White/Golden Light energy coming from the Source, we are calling forth the highest frequency we can bring to the person needing help.

**Balancing the glands of the body:**

Ben advocated touching and pulsating each gland with White Light energy with finger tips and instructing the gland "to normalize, balance and harmonize, and now produce everything that you should in the proper amounts, with nothing extra and nothing left out."

The **pituitary gland** hangs like a small berry in the center of the head approximately on a line drawn back from between the eyes. It is the Master gland, signaling most of the action of the other endocrine glands by releasing hormones into the blood stream. It secretes the growth hormones, governs the action of the thyroid gland and stimulates the production of insulin by the pancreas and the production of cortisone by the adrenals. It corrects stress changes in the body. It helps the hypothalamus and the kidneys to regulate the water content of the body, and it stimulates the production of egg and sperm cells in the reproductive glands. We should always stimulate and instruct the pituitary gland in concert with any other endocrine glands.

The **hypothalamus** is a sugar-cube-sized gland from which the pituitary hangs. It is not a hormonal gland, but seems to be one of the connectors between the chemical and neural systems. It contains the so-called "pleasure center" and is involved in the control of water metabolism in the body. It acts as the body's thermostat and internal temperature control, and produces fever when required. It contains the appestat, or appetite control, and the wake-sleep control.

The **thalamus** is slightly above and to the rear of the hypothalamus. It is not a hormonal gland but acts also as a connector between the systems. It is the reception center for touch, pain, heat and cold, and muscle sensations. Under emotion, it affects the facial muscles.

The **pineal gland** is to the rear of the thalamus in almost the exact center of the cranium, and is almost completely protected by bony structures. It emits no scientifically detectable hormones, yet it is important, being the most thoroughly protected gland in the body. It is non-automatic, but can stimulate the action of other glands (as does the pituitary) in response to the influence of Spirit or soul impetus.

The **thyroid gland** is behind the Adam's apple; its butterfly shape is wrapped around the windpipe. When it becomes overactive, it raises the metabolic rate (hyperthyroidism), which causes hot and sweaty feelings and a fast pulse, and may create a bulging of the face and throat. If it is underactive (hypothyroidism), it may slow body and brain growth, causing physical slowdown, swollen limbs and coldness, and create a tendency to anemia. One of its hormones can lower the calcium content in the blood.

The **parathyroid glands** are like little buttons imbedded in the thyroid, two to each side. If they are overactive, they will draw calcium from the bones into the blood stream and precipitate phosphate through the kidneys and pancreas. If they are underactive, the lowered blood calcium can cause prolonged twitching of the muscles.

The **salivary glands** are in a cavity above the roof of the mouth and underneath the tongue. They are not endocrine glands but, in addition to providing mucous membrane moisture, they begin digestion by enzyme action on starches.

The **thymus gland** is in the fore wall of the chest, at about its center and above the heart area. In children, this gland is quite large, but at adolescence, it shrinks. It governs the actions of the lymph glands to fight infection.

The **adrenal glands** sit atop the kidneys. They produce adrenalin and noradrenalin which affect the sympathetic nervous system. It releases other hormones to regulate the proportions of salt and water in the body and to control the carbohydrate, protein and fat metabolism. They produce cortisone, lack of which is found in arthritis. Underactive adrenal glands cause Addison's disease, low blood pressure and loss of body hair, and can affect skin pigmentation. Overactivity is associated with Cushing's disease, excessive hairiness and high blood pressure. (*I was personally having a problem with vertigo and hair loss when my soul told me my adrenals were compromised and I should take ½ a pill of hydrocortisone daily and to take larger doses of Biotin to cause my hair to thicken and regrow.*)

The **pancreas** is a combination endocrine-and-ducted gland which lies behind the stomach. The nodes on its surface, the Islets of Langerhans, produce insulin, the regulator of the sugar content of the blood. The pancreas itself produces gastric juices.

The **reproductive glands**, the ovaries or testes, are in the pelvic-pubic area. They produce estrogens and androgens (the female and male sex hormones) in both sexes. Their different balances in men and women provide the sexual characteristics. Derivatives have an effect on vitality as well as productivity.

The **lymph glands** are found throughout the body near major blood vessels. They include the tonsils. The lymph glands produce white blood cells to fight local infections. With the spleen, adrenals and pituitary, they provide hormones to reject transplants and cancer and provide valving stations to help the lymph fluid flow back upward to re-enter the bloodstream above the heart.

While they are not glands, the three locations of these organs, the liver, spleen and kidneys, need to be considered when doing the gland balancing.

The **liver** is in the right front portion of the abdomen just below the ribs, and runs around the right side to the back. It produces bile for digestion and stores carbohydrates, fats, proteins and glycogen (stored glucose). It strains the blood to eliminate nitrogenous waste products, makes albumin and globulin for blood plasma, provides clotting and anti-clotting agents and stores vitamins.

The **spleen** is behind the stomach, partially under the ribs on the left side of the back. It produces part of the white blood cells, works with the lymph glands to fight infection and destroys exhausted red blood cells (those that can no longer retain oxygen).

The **kidneys** are on either side of the backbone just at and below the ribs. They strain the bloodstream to rid it of waste products and impurities, control the balance of salt and water in the body and maintain the alkalinity of body fluids.

**Correcting menstrual problems:**

1. Meditate to arrive at the Alpha level of brain frequency.
2. Connect to the Sub-conscious or Inner Mind of the suffering person.
3. Ask their Mind to give you information about the nature of the problem.
4. Touch each gland and instruct the gland "to normalize, balance and harmonize and now produce everything that you should in the proper amounts, with nothing extra and nothing left out."
5. In dealing with difficulty during menstrual periods and the transition of menopause, it is important to do a complete hormone balancing of all the hormone producing glands. Ben placed his hand on the sufferer's head, then sent White Light energy from her head down through the body to the ovaries. He instructed the glands to balance and harmonize with all other glands in the body and to release necessary hormones in the proper amounts, and none that are not necessary. He instructed the Inner Mind to continue the treatment until the irregular condition or pain no longer existed.

**How to relieve the pressure of a migraine headache:**

In migraine headaches, the primary cause of pain-creating pressure is glandular imbalance. This could involve two or three glands, but more often you will find five or six to be involved. The need is to balance the entire upper glandular system.

1. Meditate to relax and put your Mind in the Alpha level of frequency.
2. Make visual contact with the Inner Mind of the sufferer, and then proceed to relieve pain by streaming White Light healing energy in one ear and out the other, to be followed by streaming Blue Light calming and pain-relieving energy in the same manner.
3. When you are confident the sufferer is experiencing some relief from pain, proceed to the next step. This is to balance and bring into harmony the following glands: pituitary, thalamus, hypothalamus, thyroid and thymus glands. You may mentally touch each gland, send Blue Light peace-producing energy to each in turn, and then tie the pineal gland to the connected group.
4. Instruct the pineal gland to take charge and continue with all necessary energy corrections until the entire group is completely and properly balanced and functioning normally.
5. Finally, bathe the entire head with Blue Light energy to calm all nerves and relieve tension. Continue this Blue Light energy flow until the person relaxes and all pain is gone.

**How to remove a tumor or growth:**

1. After reaching the Alpha level through meditation, proceed to make contact with the person's Inner Mind, and then check the size and location of the growth.
2. Apply shrinking energy or shrinking paste to the growth.
3. Pluck the growth out by using your fingers.
4. Fill the space where the growth was located with green healing tissue paste.
5. Cover the area where your fingers entered the body with Human skin tape.
6. Fill the person's body with Golden/White Light energy.
7. Demand that the body raise its frequency to speed the healing.
8. Mentally take the removed substance away and burn it.

**Healing hepatitis or inflammation of the liver caused by toxins or alcohol:**

1. Go into meditation to take your own Mind into the Alpha level of consciousness.
2. Observe the person's liver and determine its condition.
3. Regardless of the cause, the first step is to wash the liver thoroughly with White/Golden Light energy.
4. If you discover infection, seek out the virus or germs causing it and destroy them with White Light energy, or just command them to leave the system of the sufferer.
5. After washing it thoroughly, flood it with soothing, cooling, pain-reducing Blue Light energy. This will ease the inflammation and calm the pain.
6. Instruct the Inner Mind of the person to employ this energy in the best possible way to correct the malfunction and to redo the treatment every twenty-four hours.
7. When I observe cirrhosis of the liver, I see white snowflake-like shapes on the surface of the liver. I scrape these away gently before flooding the exterior and interior with White/Golden Light energy.

**Healing bladder, kidney and prostate malfunctions:**

1. Go into meditation to take your own Mind into the Alpha level of consciousness.
2. Observe the kidney and groin area of the person suffering.
3. Create a spray bottle filled with White/Golden Light healing energy and proceed to mentally spray it into the kidneys, bladder or prostate to wash out pus or infected debris in these organs. Instruct the kidneys to take the infected material out through urination.
4. Bathe the kidney/bladder/prostate area with Blue-Light-soothing, pain-killing energy. Cover the prostate with shrinking energy as well as the Blue Light energy.
5. Charge the person's body with instructions to raise the entire body vibration by fifty percent.

**Healing a toothache:**

1. Meditate to take your Mind vibration to the Alpha level of consciousness.
2. Connect to the Inner Mind of the person to be helped.
3. Locate the offending tooth.
4. Remove the tooth with your fingers.
5. Wash the tooth with disinfecting energy and wash the space where the tooth fits into the gums with disinfecting energy.
6. Fill the space where the tooth will be with Green and Blue (Turquoise) Light healing energy paste and replace the tooth, seating it into the paste.
7. Fill the entire mouth and head with Blue Light healing energy to stop the pain.
8. Ask the Inner Mind of the person to redo the procedure hourly until the person can get to a dentist.

**Correcting Spinal Problems:**

1. Meditate to take your Mind vibration to the Alpha level of consciousness.
2. Make contact with the Inner Mind of the person suffering back pain.
3. Look at the spine and examine its condition. If you find an inflamed area, pack this area with Blue paste and healing energy to calm the inflammation.
4. If you find a disc that is damaged or protruding: Remove the disc, create any adjustments that need to be made (if it is cracked, use mental golden glue to repair the crack) and replace it into its rightful place. If the disc is protruding, remove it and fill the space between the discs with Turquoise Light energy, rebuild the disc with Human putty and reseat it appropriately.
5. If the spine is misaligned, after filling the spinal column with Blue Light pain-relieving energy, straighten the spine to the appropriate curvature and place an energy cushion between each vertebra.
6. If there are calcium deposits on any of the vertebrae, file these away with a mental emery board or mental sandpaper and rub golden healing oil where the deposits were located.
7. Run Blue Light energy and White Light energy up and down the

entire spine.
8. Instruct the person's Inner Mind to continue sending the healing Light up and down the spine until the spine is completely healed.
9. Instruct the Inner Mind to raise the frequency of the entire body by fifty percent.

**Clearing a Poison Ivy, Poison Oak or an allergic rash:**

1. Meditate to clear your Mind and to take your Mind to the Alpha level of consciousness.
2. Connect to the Inner Mind of the sufferer.
3. Observe the rash and determine the cause of the inflammation. Wash the area with non-stinging disinfectant liquid.
4. Create a paste of bicarbonate of soda, mentally make it blue, and then gently apply the substance to the area that is inflamed or irritated.
5. Instruct the Inner Mind of the sufferer to redo the treatment every six hours until the healing is complete.
6. Instruct the person's Inner Mind to raise the overall frequency of the body by fifty percent.

**Healing Anemia and other blood diseases:**

In most cases, the problem lies in an overproduction of white cells in the blood. Overzealous activity of the cannibal section of the spleen, which under normal conditions destroys only those red cells which can no longer carry oxygen, can be causing the problem.

1. Determine if the blood condition is a result of the glandular system being out of balance, an infection, a virus, or bacteria.
2. Depending upon your findings, first clear the blood by installing a filter to capture and destroy any virus, infection or debris. The filter will also destroy the virus, infection or debris with White Light energy.
3. Anchor the person's body by grounding the body into the magnet at the core of the Earth to strengthen the iron in the person's blood.
4. Instruct the Inner Mind of the sufferer to continue to balance the systems to create the appropriate balance between the production of red and white cells.
5. Instruct the Inner Mind of the sufferer to raise the overall frequency of the person's body by fifty percent.

**Correcting diabetes and ailments of the thyroid and pancreas:**

Diabetes is usually regarded as a slowdown or failure to function on the part of the insulin-producing nodes on the pancreas called the Islets of Langerhans. It can sometimes be traced to the pituitary gland in the head which signals the Islets of Langerhans to release insulin into the bloodstream. The insulin acts as a control of the glucose (blood sugar) level in the bloodstream. As the blood sugar level becomes higher than normally required, the insulin causes a reaction in the liver which extracts the excess glucose and stores it (as glycogen) until needed.

1. Meditate to attain the Alpha level of consciousness in yourself.
2. Connect to the Inner Mind of the sufferer.
3. Observe the condition of the glands of the person's body.
4. Balance all the glands through the method previously described.
5. Directly stimulate the glands and the pancreas and its surface nodes to produce more insulin in the perfect quantity needed by this body.
6. Ask the Inner Mind to continue this treatment as long as needed to gain and maintain harmony between the glandular systems.

## 3.

# Sound Healing

"The universal vibratory energies were called by the ancient Egyptians, the Word of the Words of their gods; to the Pythagoreans of Greece they were the Music of the Spheres; and the ancient Chinese knew them to be the celestial energies of perfect harmony." (David Tame)

Our voices can be healing or hurtful depending on the tone we use. Using our voices in a positive way takes us into our heart center.

Toning is a method of using our voices to raise our vibrations, to heal ourselves and others. It is an ancient spiritual technique that is very centering. Done vocally, it creates harmonics that calm the Spirit and still the Mind. Toning is the use of the voice as an instrument of healing. Sound bypasses the intellect and has the inherent ability to trigger the emotions. There is nothing better than music as a means for uplifting the soul.

For many years I was turned off by music. Being from another planet and working in space, I was used to celestial music which has more notes and is more melodic. Shortly after I moved to Oklahoma City and was in the depths of depression, I somehow heard James Taylor sing *You've Got a Friend* and Gordon Lightfoot sing *Rainy Day People*. I was so moved by both songs that I bought the albums and listened to them over and over and over. They helped me to get back to my true self. I'm still not a big fan of music; usually, it just sounds like noise to me and I find it irritating and prefer silence.

I AM amazed by how tuned in to music my children are and how affected they are by it. Most of the people I know prefer music to silence. I often feel there is something wrong with me that I don't seem to "get it." I have an admiration for people who are musical because it seems like a foreign language to me. My soul had me buy a piano, which I dutifully did.

I took lessons for a few months, but my body never attuned itself to the sounds of the keys and how to put them together, so I gave up. Maybe in the future someone from the soul will show up to play through me the way they paint through me.

I do not have a singing voice, nor do I understand what pitch means, or being off key. In the third grade the choir teacher asked me to just move my mouth and not to try to sing. The fact that I don't understand pitch makes my body a good instrument for toning because it is something that you can't do wrong. You are not trying to hit a certain note or frequency, you are letting it happen through you from your soul.

Everything is sound, taught the ancient wisdom traditions. God created the Earth with "the Word" according to the Bible. Creation, the Cosmos and the World are all based on sound according to ancient wisdom.

The staple of shamanic traditions is to "journey" using drums or flutes. At one point in my life my soul instructed me to get a drum. Well, not being musical, I wasn't too swift at going out to find one and procrastinated. One day the phone rang and it was a man from Montana. He indicated that his soul had asked him to make me a drum. I was impressed. When I asked how much it would cost, he indicated that it was his job to make it and bring it to me in Colorado, then to have a pipe ceremony to invoke the Spirit of the drum. I was more than a little skeptical, but tried to keep an open Mind, so I asked when he would be bringing it. He indicated that he had to hunt and kill the elk, skin it to get the hide and hair that were necessary to make the drum properly, so it could be as long as a month. I agreed and pretty much immediately put the idea out of my Mind. However, about six weeks later, he called to tell me he was on his way to Colorado with the drum and asked to come where I was staying to perform the ceremony.

We sat on the floor in my friend's basement and he lit his pipe and asked me to hold the drum by putting my fingers through the webbing on the back side of the flat drum. It is about 15 inches across, and by his tradition, the hide strips had to be one continuous strip of hide from the elk. I held the drum and had no idea what to expect. He asked me to begin to drum. I very tentatively began to drum. He said, "Now I will invoke the Spirit of the drum." As he began to chant, the drum and the mallet, which was made from a stick with a round piece of hide stuffed with hair attached to the end, began to take on an energy all their own. I was drumming faster and faster without being in control or trying. Energy was pulsing through my body like crazy. I'm sure my eyes were wide open in astonishment. When he stopped chanting, the energy ceased as did the drumming. I thanked him and he left.

I later learned from my soul that I AM a member of a galactic organization referred to as the Sisterhood of the Shield. When a person remembers their connection to this organization, which is made up of a body of ancient women who look like representatives of the various Indian tribes, including Eskimos and Aborigines, an instrument of some sort suddenly comes into their lives. Sometimes it is a flute, a rattle, a drum, or they use their voice for chanting or toning. The Sisterhood sends a vibration out to its members when there is a major need for a large amount of energy to be created suddenly to avert a catastrophe or to accomplish a universal goal. In my experience the call does not come very often.

Shortly after I received the drum, I was staying in Mt. Shasta, California when I was awakened before sunrise by a sound inside my head that I recognized as the Sisterhood calling me to action. The action they requested was that I go into the redwood forest near Eureka, California, to tone and drum for several hours. The problem was a massive male frequency energy that was headed for the Earth from Uranus which, if it was not mutated and transformed as it came to the Earth, could set off another World War. I did as was suggested. As the energy came into the trees, it was blue, then became white as it radiated down each tree before it entered the Earth. If you saw the movie *Powder,* you saw a similar scene of this type of energy.

I mentioned recently in a newsletter about the Spiritual Gift of Discernment being one of the gifts available to us from the Creator. Some of the other Spiritual Gifts are the Gift of Tongues and the Gift of Sound Production. I resisted both of these, but the soul was persistent. I finally acquiesced to allow the tones and languages to come through me when I witnessed what could happen energetically when I allowed the toning and galactic languages to come through me.

I allowed myself to get on my knees in front of people I was reading for, or activating if I saw they had etheric capsules in their knees. I had learned this meant they were bringing in spiritual secrets they knew in other lifetimes.

You may feel resistance at first to the idea of toning or chanting, but I encourage you to give it a try. Try it when you are alone or maybe even in your car or the shower. You can tone **a, e, i, o, u** if you need some structure to begin with.

It is important that we now create sound circles of people who tone together to raise their vibrations and the vibrations of the Earth. Once people understand that whatever tones want to come through are correct, that there is no way to tone that is wrong, wonderful energies can be created through a group. If the group is not comfortable with generic toning, they can all tone the sound of OM or "*Om-mani-padme-hum*."

Barbara Marx Hubbard said, "I believe that music, sound and auditory vibration make up a critical factor in the graceful path to the next stage of evolution."

I believe these sound circles will move us into greater stages of consciousness and speed up Human evolution. I see healing circles of sound—large, amphitheater-size circles—in which we gather to hold flickering candles and tone together. The circle is an old and Universal symbol, having power and motion in both the physical and spiritual realms. It is the archetypal symbol for wholeness. There is a reason that units of sound are named waves. Toning can wash us clean of our angers, fears, frustrations and anxieties if we allow it and intention it. What will nurture the creative vision necessary to turn around a World possibly heading towards its own destruction? Music and toning.

Let the toning happen from your soul, from your heart.

Julia Cameron wrote this in her wonderful book The Vein of Gold.

*Just trust your heart.*
*Trust where it's taking you.*
*Just trust your heart.*
*Trust what it's making you.*
*Just trust your heart.*
*Trust that it's taking you home.*
*Just trust your song.*
*Trust what it's bringing you.*
*Just trust your song.*
*Trust that it's ringing true.*
*Just trust your song.*
*Trust that it's bringing you home.*

Sound healing is simply using sound consciously. The body perceives sound for what it is: energy. Sound uses energy to heal whatever bad energy our body is holding or experiencing. Bad energy makes itself felt first as a sense of dis-ease, and later as disease. Our own voice, used therapeutically, can heal what ails us and others.

When I do activations for people, it is necessary for me to tone, and for me to get down on my knees and tone into the knees of people who carry spiritual secrets in capsules in their knees to break up the capsules and to release the information into their bloodstream. Agreeing to get down on the floor to perform this service took a big hit to my ego.

Since time began, priests, healers, shamans, mystics, medicine men and magicians of all persuasions have been aware of the power of specified verbal formulae, spoken or sung out loud, or intoned silently within. Toning out loud is certainly more powerful than humming, but humming will also raise your vibration.

FREQUENCY + INTENTION = HEALING

Music is the heart's native language. We speak it in bliss and in grief. We speak it intuitively and unconsciously. For many people, sound is a natural tool. What do we do when a baby fusses? We croon to it.

Plato said: "Music has the capacity to touch the innermost reaches of the soul and music gives flight to the imagination."

Toning is the process of making vocal sounds for the purpose of balance. Toning sounds are sounds of expression and do not have a precise meaning. It can link one to the cosmic symphony, the music of the spheres.

**MUSIC ASSOCIATED WITH THE 49 RAYS OF GOD**

- Pomp and Circumstance
- Music only of Onward Christian Soldiers
- Chariots of Fire
- Colors of the Wind
- Candle in the Wind
- Handel's Messiah
- Peruvian Flute Music
- Vivaldi
- Music only of Battle Hymn of the Republic
- Beethoven's Fifth Symphony
- When the Saints Go Marching In
- Straus's Waltzes
- Music only of Seventy-six Trombones
- Bach's Fugues
- Rhapsody in Blue
- Amazing Grace
- Music of the Night from Phantom of the Opera

All music channeled by Hildegard of Bingen – Feather on the Breath of God
Mozart's Concertos
Pachelbel's Cannon in D
The Age of Aquarius
Music of the Beatles
Chopin's Concertos
Music from the movie Fantasia
Elephant Walk by Henry Mancini
Halleluiah and Gloria
Music from Peter and the Wolf
Music of John Williams
Indian drumming
Music of Hayden
Rock and Roll music of the 50's
Music of Tchaikovsky
The Way We Were
Some Enchanted Evening
Greensleeves
Danny Boy

# 4.

# How I Learned About The Silva Method

Shortly after I began to communicate with my soul, I began to doubt if what I was receiving was from my soul because many of the messages did not make logical sense to me. (I have since learned that Spirit is seldom logical or efficient, in my way of thinking.) I challenged my soul, that, if what I was receiving was indeed coming from my soul that I needed a concrete sign. The next message indicated, "When you encounter a huge bronze triangle held aloft by three spires of granite you will learn to transcend time and space." Well, I wasn't interested in transcending time and space; I only wanted to make sure I was actually communicating with my soul.

One Friday evening a man I had recently met at a Methodist singles group called and invited me to attend a psychic fair with him the next day. I told him I did not want to have anything to do with anything psychic. He replied that I didn't really understand what it meant to be psychic and that the word psyche actually refers to a person's soul. He dared me to go, so the next morning I met him at a local college to attend the fair. The first session of the fair was a video about Kirlian photography, a way of photographing the energy around a person or object. It was scientific and provable, and it got my attention that there might be more to being psychic than fortune telling.

The smell of incense coming from the vendor room was causing my head to stop up and ache, so I suggested that before we went through that room, that we step outside and get some fresh air. My friend obliged and we went out into the quadrangle of the college. In the middle of the quadrangle was a huge bronze triangle suspended by three huge spires of granite. I almost passed out and wet my pants. Here was concrete proof I was communicating with my soul.

We went into the vendor's room and I picked up brochures for *Touch for Health*, The Silva Mind Control Method and The A Course in Miracles before I made my apology and left the fair. I was feeling overwhelmed and headachy from the incense. I was catching a flight to Houston that afternoon to visit a friend there who had sent me a ticket. When I entered the airport gift shop, the paperback book rack was right in front of me and there was a copy of *The Silva Mind Control Method*. In the early 1980's this was not traditionally the kind of book that would be on display in an airport. I got goose bumps and bought the book. I read it on the plane and my soul indicated that they were interested in my taking the course right away. I was to stay in Houston for a week. After the first two days of my stay I explained to my friend that I really needed to get back to Oklahoma City to get a job. He was a police officer and I did not feel comfortable trying to explain what was happening with the soul messages or that I needed to return home to take *The Silva Mind Control Method* immediately. I used the excuse that I needed to get back and find a job. He understood and changed my ticket and took me to the airport.

When I arrived in Oklahoma City, I called the number on the Silva flyer and asked how much the class cost, and if they took credit cards and when I could take it. The woman who answered said they did take credit cards and the cost was $495 which was going to max out one of my credit cards. She said I would have to wait a month to take the class because they were in the middle of a two-weekend class and would not be offering the full class again for a month. I told her that my soul was insisting that I join this particular group and take the class now. I asked if she could teach me what these people had already learned between now and Saturday so I could join this group. She replied that they never taught private classes. I gave her my number and asked her to call me if she changed her mind.

She called back after she had meditated and said she was told to make an exception and to bring everything to my apartment to teach me the first two days of information. I found the class fascinating. It seemed in some ways to expand on the information my soul was giving me through direct communication. It used the same format I had been using from the *Psychic Energy* book my soul had thrown off the shelf for me at the Walden's bookstore. By doing the 3-3-3, 2-2-2, 1-1-1 and 10-to-1 meditations José teaches, I was able to get to the Alpha level easily, and learned to go inside the bodies of other people to check out their health and to leave my body to travel to other places.

A few weeks later, José was going to be in town teaching the Silva

Method of Healing and I was asked by my soul to attend, which maxed out my other credit card. I made amazing connections during that class. I met a man who financed the racks for me to expand my greeting card company and paid off my credit cards. I also met a man who became my next husband for a marriage that lasted for nine months. I've used the meditation daily through the years and it has assisted me greatly in expanding my spiritual awareness.

## JOSÉ SILVA - THE BICAMERAL MIND

(Bicameral mind means using both the right and left brain.)

*A few months ago, right after Saint Germain invited me to write the Self-Mastery book with him, José Silva came into my meditation and asked that his methods, plus what he has learned since he moved into Spirit, be included in the book.*

The discovery of the new science of *Psychorientology* by José Silva led to the creation of a Mind Control Program. Psychorientology means (1) to help to reinstate the mind to its own Inner World; that is, its own native dimension; (2) to continue to guide, direct and educate its functioning within this dimension; (3) to develop, increase and control its psychic perceptions which comprise those sensations proper to the Mind; and (4) to continue this education for further growth and development in psychic applications. By making these applications, the Mind learns to use its own field of sensation with at least the same facility with which it presently uses the field of biological sensation. One of the most important discoveries resulting from the research in Psychorientology is subjective communication, the ability of one's Mind (The Master Sense) to detect information impressed on another Mind at a distance.

He states, "The discovery that Human Intelligence can learn to function with awareness at Alpha and Theta frequencies of the brain will go down in history as the greatest discovery of Humankind. This discovery is sure to change our concepts of Mind, Psychology, Psychiatry, Psychoanalysis and Hypnoanalysis and of the Sub-conscious. Practitioners of meditation who gain alpha and theta levels of brain frequency can sense information by means other than through the five physical senses. At these frequencies, it is possible to make stronger impressions on one's brain cells and thereby retain the information they have read or heard."

José learned and taught, "This discovery indicates that the Human Brain, Mind and Intelligence functioning at these levels have tremendous problem-solving potential; it also indicates that Human Intelligence is not only capable of sensing information impressed on its own brain, but also appears to be capable of sensing information on other brains at a distance. This kind of sensing of information, when awareness is functioning at lower frequencies of a brain, is called subjective communication."

He also taught us, "The brain is like a filing cabinet; information has been stored in it since the first Human being set foot on this planet, functioning at a primitive level of animal life. This information has been passed on from father to son in many ways, including the genetic means of transmission."

The most important thing his method taught us was the technique to get into the alpha state of consciousness. Everything else he taught was a consequence of connecting to the right hemisphere of our brains by turning our eyes upward and using the counting technique to reach Alpha: Take a breath, hold it at midbrain to activate the pituitary and pineal glands, count 3-3-3 and exhale; take another breath, hold at midbrain and count 2-2-2 and exhale; take a third breath and hold it at the midbrain, counting 1-1-1 and exhale; now, breathing normally, mentally count backward from ten to one. If we keep our thumb and first two fingers of both hands together as we go into the meditation repeatedly, it trains our brains that we want to go to Alpha. When we put our fingers together in this way, even when we are not in meditation, our brain would go to the frequency of Alpha.

Coming out of meditation:
The Silva Method for coming out of meditation is to say mentally, "I am going to count from 1 to 5. When I reach 5, I will open my eyes, feeling wide awake, feeling fine and in perfect health, better than before…1, 2, 3, 4, 5, eyes open, wide awake, better than before. And this is so."

José mentioned, "Scientists have been studying the brain electronically. In the waking state, the electrical pulsations of the brain are at their highest, over 14 cycles per second. In deep slumber, these pulsations are slowest, around 0.5 to 3.5 per second. Brain wave researchers have divided these pulsations into four frequency bands, from lowest to highest: Delta, Theta, Alpha and Beta. The five physical senses: Touch, Taste, Smell, Hearing and especially Seeing are associated with the Beta level of brain functioning. Apparently, all information impressed through our physical senses is filed in some sub-compartment within Beta."

In his research and teaching, José learned to project and to teach that a Human can learn to project his Master Sense (The Mind) to the Alpha-producing part of the brain and function from that perspective with awareness. The Alpha producing part of the brain is a dimension within itself, apparently a dimension which has been neglected in Humanity's evolution. The Alpha dimension has as complete a set of sensing faculties as the Beta dimension does. Since we have not been using the Alpha dimension with awareness, we now need to orient the Psyche (Mind). With development of Mind control proficiency a person can sense, whenever there is a need, information not available through the five physical senses.

In José's teaching, he recommended that we imagine and create a laboratory where we would mentally take the etheric bodies of the people we were working on to send healing energy. We were to include in the library golden oil, as well as many devices we imagined that could assist us with the healings just as Ben Bibb had. He taught us to separate our consciousness from our body to check out the body of a person at a distance to ascertain any abnormalities in the person's body, and to use these substances and devices mentally to assist the person to heal themselves.

José recommended visualization. He now knows that to visualize, one has to lower their vibration to the Third or Fourth dimension, and that it is better to keep our vibration high and to imagine rather than to attempt to visualize. The ability to hear spiritually would also require us to lower our vibration to the Fourth or lowest part of the Fifth dimension. It is better to ask our soul for knowingness and to keep our vibration high in order to receive the information from our soul through telepathy rather than to demand a voice. When we receive knowingness, it is as clear and complete as if we saw, heard and felt the situation or object.

He taught us how to separate our consciousness to observe events happening in other Earth locations. He now wants to include how to separate our consciousness so we can take our consciousness and etheric bodies into other dimensions by the same method.

He taught us to invite guides into our laboratory to help us with the diagnosis and healing. I invited Saint Francis and Joan of Arc. To my surprise, they had never met each other, and when they first came into my laboratory they went to a corner and enjoyed meeting each other and conversing, and completely ignored me. I later learned that it was better and more useful to invite other higher levels of my Oversoul to be my guides in my laboratory. José now recommends that our guides be beings only from our own Oversouls.

He also recognizes that he did not include or teach psychic protection. He now agrees with my soul about how important grounding and protection are by sealing the room we are in on the North, South, East and West, the ceiling and the floor from any negative influence, energy or entity before we meditate and before we leave our bodies to travel into other dimensions or areas.

He taught us that we could retrain our Sub-conscious Minds while we were in Alpha to correct habits and replace self-sabotaging beliefs by inserting new beliefs.

## GROUNDING PROCESS

This process will take about two minutes each morning and begins to create a cocoon or barrier of protection between yourself and other people and other dimensions, other than the information coming directly to you from your soul. It removes the static. It also protects you from astral-plane interference and possible possession by astral entities. If you catch yourself behaving empathically during the day, stop and redo the process.

In a standing position, take a deep breath and focus on the soles of your feet. As you exhale, deliberately intention beams of energy about the size of fluorescent light bulbs (or Luke Skywalker's light saber) going from the soles of your feet into the central core energy of the Mother Earth, or see yourself as a tree with roots going into the center of the Earth.

Take another deep breath and, as you exhale, focus on your heart, deliberately opening your heart in love and appreciation to the Earth, to your physical body and to your Oversoul (God, the sky, the Universal Life Force Energy, or whatever image works for you.)

Take another deep breath and, as you exhale, open the crown of your head and have the intention of deliberately sending a beam of energy, about the size of a fluorescent light tube, from your heart, through your high heart, through the point of your mid-brain into the Cosmic-Christ-Consciousness level of your own Oversoul. (Or send the beam of energy to the Sun or to God, or whatever image works for you.)

Continuing to breathe deeply, begin to swing your arms gently at your sides, to and fro, back to front, as if you are pumping energy up from the Earth. After about one minute, change your focus to above your head and begin to pump energy down from your Oversoul. As you pump, you want to also intention pumping up balloons of energy around your body. The first balloon is white and is about twelve feet in all directions from the body; the second balloon, which is pink and inside the first, is about eight feet in all directions from the body; the third balloon is purple and is about four feet in all directions from the body. The purple balloon becomes your personal energy supply, impenetrable by others. The white and pink energy fields are excess energy, which you can afford to share with others. Very few people on the planet are spiritually adept enough to penetrate your personal energy field if you use this system.

He José also did not recommend, but now does, calling forth the Violet Flame of Transmutation, the use of the Rays, or calling forth the Blue Light of Protection which he now highly recommends.

One of the things taught in the Silva Method that I have found very useful is the glass-of-water technique. When we have a question we are curious about or struggling with, we can drink one half of a glass of water and notify our cells to search for the answer and to make the answer available to us within 24 hours. Upon awakening the next morning, we drink the second half of the glass of water and go about our day mindful of any way the Universe can get the information to us. This method is amazing and has served me greatly.

Another similar method that I use, which was not in José's teaching, is to get help to find objects I have misplaced. I decree, "Saint Anthony, Saint Anthony, Saint Anthony, please come around, something is lost and must be found." After the decree, my soul has taught me to make the sound HUUUUU. This usually works immediately, but sometimes the answer comes within the next 24 hours. This is especially helpful since things seem to be slipping from one dimension into another. I can look for a thing and it is not where I usually place it, so I look in many other places and still can't find it. I do the ritual and go on about my business. A few hours or days later I look in the normal place where I usually place the thing and it is now there. This situation can be very annoying if we do not understand what is happening and even if we do understand.

The ability to leave my body to check on my children has been especially useful to me during the years I travelled and they lived with their father in Texas. They were not particularly happy that I could do it and know what was happening with them. When I would call them to ask how they were, they would usually reply, "Fine," rather than telling me the truth, so it eased my mind and filled in the blanks left by their lack of communication.

## MY PERSONAL MORNING MEDITATION

This meditation is a result of using the Silva Meditation plus other things that my soul has suggested.

I deliberately seal this room on the north, south, east and west, the ceiling and the floor from any negative energy or entity. I ground myself into the magnetic energy at the core of the Earth to be stable and to strengthen the iron in my blood.

I call forth the blue light of protection for myself, Muffin, my home, car and my family. I ask to extend this protective bubble of blue light of protection from Guthrie to Norman and from Shawnee to El Reno; protection from damaging high winds, excessive rain, flooding, hail, excessive snow and ice, fire, tornadoes, earthquakes, theft, terrorism and violence.

I ask my body intelligence to normalize all of my glands to produce exactly the amount of hormones and substances my body needs to perform perfectly, no more and no less than each gland needs to produce. I ask to dissipate, dissipate, dissipate any static electricity collected in my body and to perfectly polarize my body between the north and south poles.

I open my heart in gratitude for my body, my Oversoul, my I Am Presence, my Holy Christ self, the Earth, all the animals, plants, minerals, water, fire, air and ethers, the Spiritual Hierarchy, the Intergalactic Federation, all the Angelic Realm, the Sun and the Moon, the Creator God of all Universes and the Great Central Sun at the center of our Solar System.

I ask for the Violet Flame of Transmutation to flow through the cells of my body, my Conscious and Sub-conscious Minds to remove all limiting beliefs, doubts, fears, judgments, negativity, jealousy and anger. I ask that all the cells of my body be healed and transformed to perfection.

I send a beam of energy from my heart, through my high heart and my mid-brain and into all levels of my Oversoul, my I AM Presence, my Holy Christ self, and into the Ascended Master's octave of Light.

I give my I AM Presence and Holy Christ Self dominion over my body, my thoughts, emotions and actions. I take a deep breath, hold it at the point of my midbrain with my eyes turned upward and count 3, 3, 3 and exhale. I take another deep breath, hold it at the midbrain with my eyes turned upward and count 2, 2, 2 and exhale. I take another deep breath, hold it at the midbrain with my eyes turned upward and count 1, 1, 1 and exhale. I count backward from 10 to 1 and sit quietly and wait for the telepathic messages from my soul about what is the next single thing for me to do or know for me to be in a state of Divine Grace?

When you catch yourself having a negative thought, as quickly as possible, voice the word "cancel, cancel, cancel" three times to keep the thought from registering and logging into your Sub-conscious Mind.

**Creation of a Laboratory:**
We must set ourselves within our own personalized surroundings so that we will use our preferences to gain positive effect. We may like certain colors or their combinations or have preferences for mountain scenes, the quiet of night, ocean swelling and crashing on rocky shores, or many other things that relax our Minds. Besides visual coloring and passive scenes that we may use for a setting, we can choose the size and shape of our work rooms complete with instrumentation and styling. This practice does not merely consist of imaginative decorating, but will also serve to set our Minds at ease or stimulate them in ways that will further our programming. We must exercise care in choosing what we want, for we should not select any portion of our inner places of work to please others; we are the ones who will use our own laboratories. This has a tone-setting quality that makes us feel in control of our environment. The atmosphere, full of personalized influences, will reinforce the constructive activity that we introduce into our laboratories.

**Mirror-of-the-Mind Technique:**
The Mirror of the Mind is a formula-type technique that you can use for problem solving. Create and project on your Mental Screen a full-length mirror. This mirror will be known as the Mirror of the Mind. This mirror can be mentally amplified in size to cover with its frame, a thing or things, a person or persons, a small scene or a large scene. The color or frame of the mirror can be mentally changed from blue to white. The blue frame will denote the problem; the white frame will denote the solution.

To solve a problem with the Mirror of the Mind, enter the Alpha level with the 3 to 1 and 10 to 1 method. Then project the image of the problem, thing, person or scene on your blue-framed mirror and make a good study of the problem. After making a good study of the problem, erase the problem image, change the mirror's frame to white then create and project a solution image onto the white-framed mirror. From then on any time you happen to think of the project, imagine it as the solution framed in white. The end results will be the solution. And this is so.

It can also be used for manifestation of a desire using the same method. Actually seeing yourself with the object, the person, the car, home, etc., imagine yourself and the object in the white-framed mirror.

## SILVA METHOD OF PAIN RELIEF

Pain is nature's way of saying something needs our attention. The beta way of pain relief:
1. Point to where you feel the pain, its exact location.
2. If the pain could fit into a container, what container size would be perfect for it? (Can, bottle, box, etc.)
3. If the pain had a color, what color would it be? Feel the pain. What color is it?
4. If the pain had a taste, what would it taste like? Feel the pain. How does it taste?
5. If the pain had a smell, what would it smell like? Feel the pain, How does it smell?
6. Go through Steps 1 through 5 again, noticing changes of the location, shape color, taste and smell.
7. If there is still some pain left, repeat the cycle (1-5) a few more times if necessary until the pain can no longer be located or felt.

Pain is a subjective feeling from the right brain. When you make an object out of it with location, shape, color, taste or smell, it then objectively can no longer be pain. Your brain obliges by sending endorphins there and the pain is relieved.

Some pain is with us for so long, we get possessive. We call it, "My pain." To hold on to it better, we give it a handle, "My arthritis pain." Break the habit. If you have a pain, do the cycle over and over.

Outside of phenomenally good health, other phenomenal changes are bound to take place as we all learn how to go to Alpha and to use both brain hemispheres in controlled ways.

You can read more about the Silva Method in books by José Silva:
*Man the Healer*
*The Silva Mind Control Method for Business Managers*
*The Silva Method of Mental Dynamics*

I personally consider my soul having me take Silva courses to be some of the greatest gifts I've given myself in this lifetime.

# 5.

# Resonance and Intuition

Webster defines "resonance" as vibrating sympathetically in response to vibrations of a particular frequency from another person or object. We are attracted to people and things that vibrate at the same frequency that we do. If we are confused, afraid, anxious, worried, angry, feeling guilty, feeling jealous, feeling judgmental or ill, our frequency of resonance will be low. If we are joyful and happy, our frequency will be high. This is why it is so important to watch what we are thinking and feeling. If we think of disturbing things that are going on in the World rather than being in a state of gratitude for what is going right in our own lives and the World, we lower our resonance and, therefore, lower our resistance to disease and accidents. Fear sets up a barrier that keeps positive things, including healing, from being able to get through to us. Guilt is insidious. Feel guilt for one minute, realize it is a result that you have just done something that is against your own basic moral belief, correct the circumstances to the best of your ability, commit to not repeating the offense, apologize and move on with your life.

In manifesting objects and people into our lives, it is important to remember what will come to us will match and resonate with our current vibration.

Conscious connection to Spirit creates safety. We are never alone. Our connection to the abiding love of God is not a talisman against calamity, but it is our true protection, even when we feel ourselves in the "valley of the shadow of death." "Be still and know that I AM God."

## bj King

> Be empty of worrying
> Think who created thought!
> Why do you stay in prison
> When the door is so wide open?
> Move outside the tangle of fear-thinking.
>
> – Rumi

Believing in things such as the practice of black magic or voodoo makes it possible for anyone practicing these arts to be able to attack us. If we are conscious of our own energy and make an effort to strengthen our own energy field through meditation, controlled breathing, direct soul contact, singing, chanting, praying, gratitude, learning a new skill, being constantly fully present to what we are doing, being in nature to develop feelings of awe and wonder and/or thinking positive thoughts, we are resonating above the frequency of anyone attempting to harm us energetically, mentally or physically.

Several dimensions of reality impinge on us constantly whether we are aware of them or not. The pull of gravity keeps our feet on the planet while the mystery of the dark matter and dark energy of the Universe penetrates every aspect of our inner and outer lives. We also cannot describe or discern the impact of what can neither be seen nor measured. Existing outside of the electromagnetic spectrum, this unknown stuff is a huge part of us, everything around us and everything far away from our planet. Each planet in our system projects energy toward the Earth. Therefore, we are affected astrologically. The phases of the Moon affect our bodies and emotions because our bodies are made primarily of water. If we make an effort to keep our vibrations high, we are less affected by any outside influence that is lower than our own vibration.

It is important to control our own thoughts and to exercise our brains. Exercise, meditation to strengthen soul contact with the body, and developing fine motor skills improves the brain's function. Exercise is the number-one activity that promotes the formation of new connections in the brain. Playing physical solitaire with a deck of physical cards improves the brain function, memory and fine motor skills. There are now some video and computer games that have proven to promote brain power, the ones that require complex decision making, skill development and rapt attention. Obviously, the ones involved in shooting and killing do not promote these skills. The capacity to change focus and direction is essential. How we move from exercise to attentiveness, from deep quiet to sensory stimulation, are all ways of building our mental capacity.

**It is important to be both relaxed and alert at all times.**

The practice of appreciation can be applied to everyday activities and perceived changes in quality of life. Studies with volunteers found that those who focused on gratitude each day, especially by writing down what they were grateful for, reported significantly happier lives. One possible biochemical explanation for these effects is that a heightened state of feeling happy through appreciation causes more dopamine to be produced in the brain that, in turn, activates areas of the brain responsible for conflict resolution and patterns of complex thinking.

**"The only real valuable thing is intuition." – Albert Einstein**

Intuition may seem nothing more than an inexplicable hunch or mysterious sense that nudges us toward certain choices or actions. There is some element of mystery to intuition; it can't be completely explained in scientific terms. We can't see intuition on a brain scan, as we can some other neurological functions and states of Mind. Scientists haven't identified where intuition lives in the brain—or even if it resides only there. There is much more to intuition than what we know.

When we look closely at the intricate mechanisms for communication and interaction between the Brain, Mind, Body and Spirit, we see that intuition is part of an elaborate internal "intelligence operation" in which cells collect, process and disseminate information constantly. Just as our sense of sight allows us to take in our surroundings, our intuitive sense continually monitors our internal and external environments, processes the information and makes it available to us in subtle ways. Intuition may alert us to a shift in circumstance or emotional energy in someone we know, or nudge us in a direction with everyday choices we make. We may follow our intuitive hunches and make highly effective choices in our work. Or we may sense an undiagnosed physical illness. The more attuned we are to our intuitive sense, the more consciously we can receive its messages and act from this deeper awareness.

It is possible to learn to listen for intuition and trust it as an expression of our authentic voice of Mind, Body and Spirit. It is possible to cultivate intuition through simple mindful living—learning to listen closely to life and nature, or through meditation, yoga or other physical and spiritual practices. For some people a sudden life crisis, serious illness or loss, brings the inner voice forward with intuitive wisdom, as it did with me.

I have learned through the years how important it is to receive my intuition through direct soul communication rather than staying open with my emotional body and reading others and my environment through my emotional body by being empathic. Remaining empathic and allowing everything that is going on within our galaxy, our universe and individually with people and the Earth itself can be overwhelming and devastating to our well-being. You can understand more about how to overcome being empathic in favor of being consciously multi-dimensional by checking out information on our blog. (namasteconsciousness.com)

When I first moved back to Oklahoma City after years of travel, I needed to find a psychic chiropractor to help me to take care of my body. After I put the request to my soul in meditation, I began to wake up every day with the song *Row, Row, Row Your Boat* in my head. I didn't understand the message. My next client was a woman I had known for years in Oklahoma City, but I had not seen her for over ten years. I felt intuitively to ask her if she knew of a local psychic chiropractor. Her response was, "Sure do. There's Jacque Rowe, Michael Rowe and Daniel Rowe. I think Jacque is the more psychic of the three. He works with the Spiritual Hierarchy." I had to laugh at my soul's sense of humor. Intuition isn't always obvious. Sometimes we have to figure out the message or develop a language of symbology between our Conscious Mind and the intuition the soul gives us. We all need to fine-tune the way our intuitive sense processes incoming information and delivers it to us. Deliberately going into an altered state of awareness by controlling our breathing to slow the brain frequency to reach the Alpha level of brain wave frequency when we are seeking an intuitive response from our soul is useful.

Reflect on a particularly successful action you took in your life. How much did you rely on your analytical skills? How much did your intuition contribute? Allow yourself to realize and appreciate how you can combine intuition and analysis to make your life more successful.

Listen for these qualities; they can help you to discern between true intuition and impulsive or ego tendencies:

<u>Neutrality</u>: Intuition is impartial. A neutral state of Mind allows intuition to emerge freely. When we are pushing for a particular outcome, attached to a result, or grasping at a specific option as the only way, we are unable to hear the deeper inner voice of intuition over the cacophony

of other input. Neutral does not imply that you do not care, but that you trust a higher order to guide you to the most effective outcome. We can create our neutral place of listening in the moment, anywhere, simply by choosing to set aside the noisy voices of intense attachment to outcome for a few moments of quiet reflection and neutrality. Your intuition is on your side; if you are to act effectively in the complexity of circumstance, your actions need to be precise, limited and valuable. Intuitive actions are that.

<u>Physically</u>: More often than not, I feel the nudge of intuition in a physical sense. If I am drawn toward something visually, like a book or an object the soul is interested in my taking home with me, it is almost like the object lights up; not really, but the resonance matches mine and, therefore, I know it's mine. When I first began working with Spirit, when something was important for me to pay attention to, I would get an electrical impulse in my upper right thigh. I thought maybe my veins were breaking, since I had no one to talk with at that time about what was happening. Also, when my soul had a message for me, I would get a ringing in my right ear, and when the message was coming from the federation, the ringing would be in my left ear. I've evolved to the point where my body resonates with the eighth level of my Oversoul so the messages come in more like knowingness and less like intuition. I highly recommend asking your soul for direct knowingness.

"Easy" is not a sensory experience that necessarily connotes correct intuition. As I've said before, in working with your soul, what is indicated by your intuition may be something you don't want to do or seems too difficult. Remember you have Freewill and can always negotiate with your soul. When an intuitive message suggests something hard or unwanted, write out conditions under which you would attempt what is being suggested. If the conditions begin to be fulfilled by the Universe, you know what is being asked of you is important to the soul or to the overall quality of your life.

<u>Spirituality</u>: One of the most reliable ways to enhance your intuitive knowing is to continue your spiritual practice. In embracing spirituality as a source for intuitive guidance here are three key aspects:

1. How we see ourselves and how we imagine the Universe. How am I in this moment? How do I experience my connection with the nature and the flow of all things? Am I acting in accord with my deepest spiritual intuition?
2. Is my meditation vital to my everyday life? Does my meditation grow and change as I develop spiritually? Am I willing to allow my

meditation to shift from duty to delight? How are my meditative experiences informing my intuition?
3. Is my life in the workplace and with my family congruent with my spirituality? Do I cherish the flow of intuitive wisdom in the simplest of daily activities? Have I learned to listen to intuition with ease and grace in all aspects of my life?

Reality Check: Not every nudge is an accurate intuitive message. While the qualities of neutrality, and physically and spiritually listening are crucial in developing reliable intuition, it is also appropriate to check out those intuitive calls to action with another person. But ultimately it comes back to one's own deepest discernment as the .consequences of every choice, good or not so good, every choice rests on each of us individually. Check out if your intuition involves the presence of compassion and the ability of the action to serve the highest good.

When you are invited to a party, event or a trip, I recommend going into meditation and seeing if you can feel yourself being at the event or party or feel yourself at the destination of the trip. Doing this usually gives me a clear indication if the event, party or trip is to my highest good, or if the event, party or trip is even going to take place.

In everyday situations, intuitive guidance can lead us to unexpected and rewarding outcomes, missing being involved in accidents, meeting people we haven't seen in a while, meeting new people or just helping to open the door for someone trying to enter the post office with an armload of boxes because we left home at the exact time the intuition suggested.

The Human body is made up of between 75 and 100 trillion cells. This is a well-organized system, neither random nor scattered, but highly structured and efficient. The cells communicate with each other continually. Adjacent cells send out small tubes, called nanotubes, which exchange information directly, cell by cell. Our cells maintain resonance with each other and the whole body through these extraordinary means.

There is a natural arc from our cells to our brain that informs us of many of the needs of our body: time for lunch, get your hand away from the flame, time to sleep or pay attention to that pain in your knee. These are messages from the unseen World of our cells to the knowable. Yet another arc loops from subtle perception to the mystery of the spiritual dimension.

My sense is that we have a separate intelligence that I call the "body intelligence" that controls what we think of as the automatic functions of the body. The "programs" or "software" running this "computer" can become corrupted by our environment, stress, additives in the body that should not be there, or our habitual negative thought patterns. We have the ability to communicate directly with this body intelligence system through our thoughts and our affirmations to correct glitches in the software programs.

Several forms of physical energy activate our sensory systems: vibration creates sound, which our ears translate into communication; Light transmits images, which we experience as vision. All this information is passed as biochemical packets between brain cells as it shapes our perception of the World.

When we experience frustration, it blocks the access we need to our intuitive knowing. Frustration also occurs when we do not believe ourselves connected to the consciousness of the Universal Source and do not believe ourselves to be a part of God. It is important to believe and to practice the "Presence" of God within us. This "Presence" may appear to us in meditation as colors or shapes, fragrant smells, lovely music, body sensations (heavy or light feelings), temperature changes, tears or emotions. We cannot grasp or command "Presence" to come to us. It is already here within us. Belief, openness and faith help and are useful, but the grace of awareness of ourselves as part of God may bless us at any moment. The good news is that the yearning for that contact with "Presence" opens the door to practices that you can adapt in your own best way.

For each of us there is a true Self, a blessed seed of the most sacred. The connection that comes from the awareness of that Self is gentle, immediate and safe. I do not need to hope that an amulet, a certain mantra, a specific holy site, a church nave, or anything else that affords protection. The connection to Self and the Universe is sufficient. Union is a reality and our connection with God is, indeed, a safe path that leads us to communion with all that is.

Substantive spiritual connection involves developing awareness of one's own central core and confidence in one's own true nature as a spiritual being. Almost always, the answers and insights we seek are not conceptual. In other words, we cannot think our way into those answers. It took me a long time to trust that guidance and protection were all around me and that I could move into just the right place, just the right connection, without having to rationalize every step and nuance.

Our personal experience of protection and connection can begin with the way our body works. Cells are specialized and highly adapted to manage particular areas of vulnerability. Skin cells in Humans preserve our outer form and protect us from all sorts of environmental intrusion without being an immovable covering of armor. To do this, skin cells produce keratin, a tough, waterproof protein. The cells responsible for making keratin are called keratinocytes. One attribute of keratinocytes is their ability to enlist other cells for protection when needed. They can mount their own form of immune response to a scratch or cut and can signal a full inflammatory response. The fibers are also waterproof and make the whole skin surface water resistant. Just think what it would be like if your skin were more like a sponge.

Compassion is not a static quality; it leads to action. Compassion can be expressed in words, facial expression, body language and total silence. Often when we visit a sick person, we can be a more comforting presence by relaxing in a connected silence with an expression of compassion which will bring comfort to an ailing person. New studies show that the normal Human brain is functionally and structurally organized to sense distress in others. Even the image of someone suffering causes specific neurons in the prefrontal lobe of our brain to fire up in a location that is known to be associated with the impulse to leap to assist. Compassion is not a generalized phenomenon; it is specific to each situation and it is especially engaged when our Minds and hearts are most clear. It is quite different in tone from pity, which often leads to stagnation and a long-lasting state of emotional sadness. Compassion looks for an outlet in the form of helping deeds. Compassion, sympathy and empathy are not the same thing. Compassion is combining our energy of passion with another individual. Sympathy lowers us to the energy level of the person suffering. Empathy connects our energy to the energy the other person is feeling. Offering compassion, we are connecting to the energy of the person's soul and raising the vibration of the situation for both ourselves and the suffering person.

# 6.

# How To Transcend Being Empathic

To be "empathic" is to consciously or unconsciously project oneself into the consciousness of another Human being, at the emotional or energetic level, in order to have sympathetic or empathic understanding of the other Human being. Many healers are empathic and read their client's body by merging with their body to feel what is going on with the client. This is against spiritual law and detrimental to the healer. After the session they will be left with an emotional residue they will pick up from the client's body.

When we were born, we trusted our instincts, but we were born helpless. We knew we had needs, the need to be warm, dry, fed and reassured that the body was going to be protected and cared for. In order to figure out how to get these needs met, we pushed our emotional bodies out and merged them with the people around us. We became empathic. At birth we have a tendency to be energetically like little amoebas. We have unstructured borders to our energy fields. We move our energy fields in and around the energy fields of other people in order to check out how they are feeling. We do this instinctively in order to know how to get what we want, in order to be safe, or in order to comprehend that which is around us. We found that if we cried someone would usually come to feed us, bathe us, put us in dry clothing and sometimes hold us, rock us, talk to us, reassure us.

As we grew older, we kept using the method of being empathic to check out our surroundings and other people so we would know how to be or behave to either get our own way, how to please other people to get positive attention, how to get our needs met or to stay safe.

Each time we merged our emotional body with that of others we came back tainted by their emotions. Each time is like blowing up a balloon and then letting out the air. Our borders become less and less well defined. Leaving our energy fields open in this way and practicing being empathic, we are like walking sponges filled with other people's feelings and opinions. This makes it more and more difficult for us to be in control of our own emotions or to even know which emotions are ours and which belong to others. Being empathic can easily lead to depression. If we don't have any conscious awareness that we are being empathic, we don't know why we feel the things we do. Often this leads a person to shut down emotionally, or to become completely unconscious of how they personally feel. They may still pick up on the feelings of others, but not be in touch with their own feelings.

Often a person who has been painfully empathic will become completely shut down emotionally, or they will be so open empathically that being in public is excruciating for them, and they will become reclusive even to the point of agoraphobia.

Many people remain empathic, never knowing if the pains and emotions in their bodies are theirs or belong to the people they have encountered. They remain ignorant that they are even picking up feelings and emotions from others and believe that all this confusion and turmoil is their own.

We are never in control of our own feelings as long as we continue to be either consciously or unconsciously empathic. An empathic person finds it very difficult to understand where they stop and other people begin. They have a tendency to allow their boundaries to be invaded by other people. They do not even understand the concept of personal boundaries. When a person is unconsciously empathic, it is difficult for them to have a good self-image. Their self-image is controlled by the thoughts other people have about them. They do not have a clear impression of selfhood and others. When a person is unconsciously empathic, the gift of being able to read other people empathically becomes more of a curse than a gift.

My own level of being empathic became so debilitating that going shopping was painful. The idea of being in a crowd of people at a movie or concert was impossible. I reached a point where, when I went to the grocery store, I would become so anxiety ridden by the time I reached the rear of the store for the milk I would have to quickly leave the store, often without buying anything. I was so open energetically that I was affected by all the emotions and thought forms left in the air by other shoppers. I learned to shop very early in the mornings after the store had been closed and cleaned, but would still have to make the trip short and only buy a few items at a time, and only buy the most immediate necessities.

I had no idea I was empathic. I didn't even know the word. I only knew I was anxious, nervous and felt afraid and out of control. I became more and more emotionally withdrawn from my family and the people who were around me on a daily basis.

The doctor I went to prescribed Valium for my nerves. Valium is a depressant and only helped me to sleep and to not shake visibly. It did not shut me off from other people's feelings. It made me less and less aware of my own feelings and I developed a feeling of "whatever" when asked a question that required an opinion about how I felt.

In 1982 I developed soul communication and found that my problem was being empathic and how to solve it by using the grounding process on page 40 88, which was given by Spirit.

After using the grounding process for a while and creating the intention within myself that I no longer desired to operate empathically, I was able to quit taking Valium and developed an awareness of my own feelings. The times of depression lessened.

Spirit later explained that unutilized creative energy is a sure cause for depression. It will make us feel unsettled, restless, discontent with ourselves and others, angry, cranky, listless, filled with fear and anxiety. Ultimately, it will lead to dis-ease, which will ultimately lead to depression, and then to physical illness. The severity of the depression and ultimate physical illness will depend on the level of our resistance to allowing the soul access to using the body. Our bodies were created to be used by our souls to have access to, and experiences in, this dimension and Earth. When we adamantly refuse this truth and live the life as if it belongs to us, the "us" that is the ego, we will suffer. More and more people are leaving their bodies. Most of the souls are retreating from the bodies in instances where the personalities refuse to acknowledge and allow soul utilization of the bodies.

When we consciously leave the soul out of our lives, we will never feel the confidence we can feel if we decide to let the soul live through our bodies. Living from the intellect alone we will always suffer from Divine discontent. If we don't know this is caused by lack of attention to our soul, we will try to assuage the feeling with food, drink, sex, television, sports, exercise, drugs, the Internet, computer games, gambling, work or travel. What we are really feeling is being cut off from our soul, our Source.

There is a reason every other ad we see on television is for an anti-anxiety drug, a drug for depression, a drug to relieve erectile dysfunction. Most of the people in the World today are operating empathically.

Most people eat in an attempt to create a barrier between themselves and others, or they have extended their emotional balloon so many times that their bodies no longer know where their natural boundaries lie. Other people attempt to shut out the feelings and noises of others by using alcohol or drugs, which actually causes them to be even more open not only to the feelings and energies of others, but makes them susceptible to possession by discarnate entities (dead people) who died in a state of addiction to drugs, sex, money, power, anger, food, alcohol, nicotine or even killing or abusing others. Being out of control of our own emotions can lead to being out of control of our bodies and Minds.

Possession, whether it is occasional, periodic (when the person uses alcohol or drugs) or permanent to the extent that the original soul aspect is no longer even present, is real. We've all seen a person have one or two drinks without becoming seriously impaired. We've also seen people who, after about the third drink, their eyes change and they've been joined by one or more discarnate entities feeding off of their use. They no longer seem to be themselves, and they are not.

When a person dies in a state of addiction, their vibration is slow, no matter what type of addiction they were practicing. Because of the addiction, they were unable to move into the Light, or a higher vibration. In Christian terms, they would not make it into Heaven. Their vibration would hold them in limbo, purgatory or what Christians would call hell; what I would call the astral plane or the Fourth dimension.

In the Fourth dimension, a person's physical body would no longer exist, but they would still have their etheric body. Their etheric body still has the addiction. Because they had no body through which to relieve the craving, they would feel they are in hell. The energies of the first three chakras (energy centers in our bodies) vibrate at the frequency of red, orange and yellow. Therefore, their etheric bodies in the astral dimension could look like "the fires of hell."

Without a physical body, they can get no relief for their urges and addictions. They seek an embodied person who is practicing their drug, addiction, or behavior of choice and they merge their consciousness and etheric body with this person to get relief from their addiction. They energetically and emotionally encourage the embodied person to carry out their preferred addiction or behavior.

An addicted person is seldom practicing an addiction just for themselves. They usually have disembodied beings encouraging them to smoke, use drugs, overeat, or abuse others emotionally, physically or sexually. They encourage anger, disagreements, sexual behavior and anything that will induce fear. Astral entities must feed their etheric bodies with the energy of fear, anger and raw sexual energy. They love to invoke anxiety and fear in individuals and groups.

Newscasters, leaders and politicians who are being influenced by astral entities will deliberately invoke fear in large numbers of people. They whip people into an energetic frenzy to the extent that the individuals no longer think for themselves but operate as a mob, which gives tremendous energy to the disembodied entities. These entities are excessively present at competitive sporting events, especially violent ones like hockey, football, wrestling and boxing. Of course, they hang out in bars, nude clubs and where prostitution is practiced. They love to influence a person to view pornography on the internet and in magazines.

If you are concerned that you have entities attached to you or someone you know, never try to confront an astral entity. You have the power to exorcise these energies or entities by using the prayer at the end of this chapter. You do not have to have the person's permission to do the exorcism, because possession is against spiritual Law. If the person continues to use drugs or alcohol, the prayer will need to be used continually for a while to give the person a chance to not be possessed or influenced by other entities, and to give them a clear space within which to make their own decision to be free of addictive influences.

The Earth's vibration is being raised; the energy and time are speeding up. Only those who agree to wake up to the true purpose of the bodies as vehicles for use by the souls will remain in the Aquarian Age. Daily we see the obituary pages expanding. Everyone knows someone who has died recently. Wars, genocide, natural disasters, diseases are removing people daily in larger and larger numbers.

When we surrender our Body and Mind to the soul and find our purpose, the purpose the soul had for creating our body, which we believe is ours, we can feel confident and actually more in control than we ever felt when we were allowing the ego to rule the life and the body.

When we surrender our and Body and Mind to the soul, we begin to feel more energy, inspiration, grace and ease. Synchronistic and serendipitous experiences begin to happen in our lives. The depression lifts and we can feel the soul guiding us into useful, fulfilling lives.

When I meet a psychic person who is reading others by being empathic, they are often resistant to the idea of giving up being empathic, believing this is their "gift" and that they must remain empathic in order to fulfill their destiny. If they are willing to trust their souls, they can reprogram themselves to receive necessary information about their clients by being consciously multi-dimensional rather than empathic. It does, however, take discipline to change our way of being energetically. When I use the word discipline, many people hear the word punishment. To be disciplined is to care enough about yourself to do whatever is to your highest good; it is a form of self-love, self-respect.

When a person is empathic, they respond emotionally, usually with tears, when large amounts of spiritual energy enter their bodies during readings or meditations. This causes discomfort for them and for their client and is not necessary.

Being empathic is against spiritual law and is intrusive and self-sabotaging. In being empathic, we are picking up information from others and carrying it for them, or acting it out for them, unconsciously. It is difficult to differentiate between what are our feelings and emotions and the emotions of others. If you have been consciously or unconsciously empathic, it is time to give up this means of accessing information about others.

Being empathic causes many people to be overweight, excessively emotional, or to become addicted to substances because of being overly sensitive. When the emotional body has no boundaries, the physical body tries to become the size of the emotional body. This feeling of being out of control emotionally leads to excessive eating in order to try to feel in control or to feel grounded. We often erroneously try to create a physical barrier between ourselves and other people since we have no emotional boundary. It is also possible, when we are not in control of our emotional bodies, to attract astral plane entities that want to feed off of our excess emotional energy. They are attracted to sexual energy, fear energy and anger or conflict energy.

If we choose to act responsibly energetically, it is time for us to give up being empathic in favor of being deliberately multi-dimensional. To do this we have to rewrite our software, our program to only seek Oversoul communication with our own Oversoul and to deliberately program ourselves to communicate with others from our Oversoul to their Oversoul. This form of communication bypasses the emotional body. When we need information about another person, we can communicate with our Oversouls, and if it is ours to know, our Oversoul will communicate with the Oversoul of the other person and the information or awareness we need will come into us in the form of intuition or knowingness.

If we agree to communicate in this way, when our soul disconnects from the other person's soul, we are not left with any feelings, diseases or emotions that rightfully belong to the other person. In this form of communication, we also bypass what is called the morphogenic field of thought that has built up over time between us and people with whom we are familiar. This field operates like a rut that develops over a period of time between people who communicate often, such as spouses, lovers, children or parents. When one person speaks to the other, the energy of information goes through the rut and the responsive party already believes they know what the speaker is going to say. They "hear" it in the way they have always heard thoughts as warped by the rut. If we go directly to our soul to communicate with their soul, the words we speak will have a different energy and we may be actually "heard" for the first time. Their soul gives us intuitive awareness of analogies and verbiage that will gain their attention.

The body is a bio-magnetic computer system for the soul. It can be reprogrammed with new software. <u>The new software is installed by intention</u>. We can cease to be unconsciously empathic by deliberately grounding ourselves each morning, by installing intentional balloons or cushions of energy around ourselves, and by having an intention to communicate telepathically, or through direct knowingness (rather than empathically) with the Oversouls of those we encounter.

The more open we become energetically, the more information we may pick up from our environment and others which is often inappropriate. In order to avoid picking up information unintentionally, it is useful to practice the previous grounding exercise on page 40 88 to reprogram our Body, Mind and Spirit. If we change our method of communication, we can choose to pick up information only when that is our intention rather than randomly.

## SPIRITUAL PROTOCOL

As psychics or mystics, it is spiritually inappropriate to invade the thought forms or psychic space of another individual without being specifically invited by that person. Deliberately tuning in to other people without being asked is equivalent to opening another person's mail, eavesdropping or listening in to the party line of a telephone. As we become more and more open, it is important for us to control our own energy space (and thoughts) and to not impinge on the energy spaces of other people. When we move in the direction of not being empathic and only getting information about a person or situation by requesting that our Oversoul communicate with their Oversoul, we are following spiritual protocol. We are not to offer unsolicited spiritual advice, nor are we to alter the energy field of another person in any way without being asked by them, or without first asking permission of their soul. To do this without permission infringes on a person's free will, which is against spiritual law.

In our zealousness, when we first begin to open up to Spirit, we have a tendency to share all of our impressions and the information we receive or perceive with other people, whether it is solicited or not. When we begin to be aware that healing energies are flowing through our bodies, we have a tendency to want to share this gift with everyone we meet who is suffering in any way. When we first learn a new spiritual tool, again in our enthusiastic state, we have a tendency to want to practice it on everyone we meet. We may justify our actions by thinking that this is to their highest good. We have no idea (unless we have checked this in the Akashic Records) why this person is having this experience and what the relevance of this experience is to their spiritual growth. Therefore, we are interfering with spiritual law if we do not wait to be asked to intercede on that person's behalf, even with prayer.

Just because we know something about another person does not mean we should speak it. It may be premature for them to know or may be emotionally distressing for them to know. Wait to be asked; do not volunteer. I observe many spiritual workers seeking to do readings, healings and procedures for people rather than waiting to be approached by individuals whose souls are directing them to have sessions through specific individuals. I see this being done sometimes from enthusiasm and sometimes because the reader or healer is suffering financial insecurity. Certain individuals are more suited than others at a given time, through which certain energies and information can be given and received. Therefore, people need to wait to be intuitively guided to a certain individual through whom they feel their soul is guiding them to receive information or healing. If a person does not wait for their intuition, but seeks advice from every psychic or healer they encounter, they will become increasingly more confused rather than clearer about their direction.

A reader or practitioner needs to have enough integrity and discernment to know, if, when an individual approaches them, if they are the correct person who is supposed to read or interact with the candidate seeking help. A reading should never be done solely because you need the money. If you refer the person to the appropriate practitioner (and you will be intuitively guided to know who they should see), then wait, you will be sent more clients than you have time to work with because of your integrity. <u>Competition between spiritual practitioners is always inappropriate.</u>

To be within Spiritual Law it is recommended that we seek to receive information only from our own Oversouls and to ask our Oversouls to contact the Oversouls of other people. We will then be given the knowledge of what is appropriate, and what we have permission to ask for the person. We will also be told if we can pass on information to them, which we are receiving from their Oversoul. Never tell your client that you are receiving information, but you are not being allowed to give them the information at this time. Do not mention this information <u>at all</u>.

It is Spiritual Law for us to become aware that every creation is sponsored and supported by a specific Angelic Presence. It is useful to seek to be in communication with that Presence when we desire to change the conditions of a structure, person, plant, animal, etc. This includes getting permission from our "body intelligence" or the "body intelligence" of another person if we or they are going to have surgery of any kind or an activation or healing.

Spiritual Guardians are assigned to groups, structures, organizations, portals and places where deliberate vortexes of energy have been set in motion. Such as a meditation group will be assigned a Spiritual Guardian in addition to the Over-lighting Devic Presence of the place where the meditation group meets. A deliberate vortex of energy will become established where a group meditates regularly. There is a Spiritual Guardian of an organization such as a Mystery School like Astara in Upland, California. This Mystery School is sponsored by the energies of the Spiritual Guardian Master Zoser, sometimes spelled Djoser. A religion, such as Unity or Religious Science, will have a Spiritual Guardian or Group Mind Guardians assigned to the organization. Each church building may have an individual Spiritual Guardian or Over-lighting Devic Presence. The Master Jesus, the Master Dwjal Kuhl, the Master Kuthumi and the Master Saint Germain are sponsoring the Namaste Mystery School of Remembering.

The Hierarchy of the Universe is complex, but it can be learned. The more we allow ourselves to be open to learn the correct rituals, procedures and structures, the more powerful our meditations and life will become. The more conscious we become, the more we can be used by our Oversouls, the Spiritual Hierarchy, and the Angels, and the Intergalactic Federation to serve our souls, the Earth, the Universe and God.

If we observe protocol by having mental intention when we enter a structure by asking to communicate with the Over-lighting Angelic Presence and the Spiritual Guardian, we will be in harmony. If we do not observe with mental intention and ritual, we will be out of harmony with the structure and with the guardians of the property. This also holds true for our homes and places of business. If we acknowledge the Over-lighting Angelic Presence of our homes, it will feel harmonious to us and to others who enter it. If we do not it will not feel as comfortable. If we honor the Angelic Presence who holds the form for our plants to grow, they will grow well, or tell us what they need, whether these plants are indoors or out.

If we enter a sacred site to do any change to the energy of the site, we should acknowledge the Guardian of the site by turning our bodies three times to the left as we would unlock a door. This acknowledges to the Guardian that we are in a state of respect and awareness or their authority. When we leave the site, we should again turn our body three times to the left to reseal the energy field of the site.

Much of this information was taught in the ancient Mystery Schools, and only handfuls of people were allowed to have access to the information and rituals. Because of the power that the knowledge causes to be available, it has been guarded until Humanity evolved to be trusted to be responsible. The same holds true with knowledge of Universal Law, knowledge of the Rays, knowledge of Angels (in all their forms including Devas) and an understanding of the Oversoul, the Intergalactic Federation, and the Spiritual Hierarchy of this planet, galaxy and Universe.

If we hold the intention of harmlessness and an intention to use information given to us spiritually with integrity, rather than for self-gain, self-aggrandizement, or to impress others, we will be given more and more information. If we misuse the information given to us by sharing it inappropriately or using it to gain power over another person physically or mentally, our gifts and access will be revoked, very much like a library card would be revoked if a person were abusing their use of the library.

A person who asks for and receives access to the Akashic Records will be given probationary access to limited amounts of information until they have proven themselves spiritually trustworthy to have access to a broader range of information. One might think again of the idea of a library (although that is not my experience of how these records or are stored). A novice reader would be given a password or library card which allowed them access to the first floor of the library where limited amounts of information, which is relatively easy to understand, are stored. As the person grows spiritually and uses the information with discretion and disseminates what they learned appropriately, they are given passwords progressively that will take them into levels which reveal more and more complex information.

We are always given information from Spirit on a "need-to-know basis". When our ego demands to know information, out of curiosity, which is not ours to know, this information is seldom accurately forthcoming. If a person persists, they may begin to access realms other than their own Oversoul, and information may be (allowed by the soul) may be given, which is either not accurate or is misleading, by entities who are mischievous or malevolent. The Oversoul allows this in order to bring forth a circumstance which will give the person an opportunity for a much-needed spiritual lesson in discernment. Trust me, this is not a fun experience. I speak from past personal experience, which is how I learned what I know about protocol and to ask only one question of the soul at all times.

## WHAT IS THE NEXT SINGLE THING FOR ME TO KNOW OR DO FOR ME TO BE IN A STATE OF DIVINE GRACE?

If we learn to live with this question, we will always have the information we need in the moment. It is best to communicate only with your own Oversoul, to accept information on a need-to-know basis and to use and disseminate that which we are given with discretion. It is best to focus on our own path and to ask for information which would be positively useful to us. Then if we feel intuitively led (not by our ego, but by our Oversoul) led to publish or share the information we've been given, a way to do so will be provided through divine right action.

If we worked in a large corporation as the mail clerk, we would not send each request we had directly to the office of the President or Chairman of the Board, we would speak with our immediate supervisor. We would, therefore, get a quick and easy-to-understand answer, which would be relevant to our position and in a language suited to our level of understanding. In my understanding and experience, the same holds true for the relationship between the various departments of the order of the Spiritual Hierarchy of this Universe.

It is useful to develop a relationship with the highest level of our souls, through the vibration of the Cosmic Christ Consciousness, that our physical bodies can tolerate at this time. In developing that relationship, that level of our Oversoul can become our gatekeeper, our spirit guide, or our receptionist, and take messages from other spirits that might desire to interact with us. If we develop this relationship, we can always trust the information we receive. Our gatekeeper can translate or interface with other spirits so that we are not constantly trying to sort through the various messages we might encounter or having to challenge each spirit that approaches us to see if they are of the Light.

After thirty-eight years of interacting with my soul, the Spiritual Hierarchy, the Intergalactic Federation, Angels and even recently dead Spirits, I offer you this information based on my experience and opinions, and in no way do I offer it as anything other than my own truth. You should always test all information you read or hear through your own discernment. If you do not feel you have discernment, pray for it. Discernment is a spiritual gift and can be gifted to you by your soul if you request it. It is important to remember the soul, Angels, and God are not able to override The Universal Law of Freewill to help us unless we first ask and give permission for their intervention.

# Book Three

# The Oversoul and Reincarnation

1.

# Multi-Dimensionality and the Oversoul

All of creation is sacred and alive. Each part is connected to each other part, and each is communicating in a cooperative effort to evolve. The smallest and the largest forms of life are involved at the cellular level and at the level of consciousness in this evolution. Our physical senses present our unique version of reality, in which our beingness is perceived in one particular dimension. Our perception of that beingness is built up through neurological patterning, and is the result of one kind of neurological focus. There are other alternate neurological routes as yet not chosen by many. Our environment, family, government and religion have established our current sequential perceptions. These perceptions have locked Humanity into certain perceptions of reality. These structures were meant to frame and organize experience, but we mistook the picture for the reality it represents. These structures demand recognition of the Third dimension as the only possible reality. Our sequential prejudiced perception can be altered, however, and is more flexible than we might imagine. At all times, other unperceived impulses bombard us. These impulses are either too fast or too slow for our usual focus to perceive them. Our recognition of these "not familiar" energies can be learned and encouraged. Many people refer to this ability as extrasensory perception. We are all designed and capable of these other-dimensional perceptions. At a certain point in Human evolution, we were designed to begin to experience what some people refer to as psychic phenomena in order to bring our attention to these other dimensional realities. That time is now.

Governments and religion try to preserve the status quo, to preserve their own existences, not for political or religious reasons, but to preserve the official picture of the self around which they are formed. Fortunately for us, the structured reality in which that kind of self can exist is breaking down. The official picture no longer fits or explains private experience. At this time, we are not only being affected by exterior conditions, but also by interior "seeds" planted by our souls, to explode at this time and to cause us to question the idea of the Third dimensional reality as being the only one, and to question Humans as being the only sentient beings in the Universe. The blueprint for Humanity's future is seeded in the tissues and the cells of the species itself.

When I first began to have these seeds explode within me, I was within the structure of organized religion. I had the focus of God, Jesus, Mary, Joseph and the unknown energy called the Holy Spirit. I had never seriously considered reincarnation, because, of course, it is not taught in the Christian religion. I had never seriously considered the soul, actually, or the difference between the soul and the spirit. I studied the *Bible*, and the more I studied, the more questions I had, which were not logically addressed by the priests and authorities. I began to question the theology and dogma of Christianity and saw it as illogical. This did not make me comfortable or popular. When the seeds began to explode so a new reality could be revealed within me, it wreaked havoc in my life, in my thinking and in my emotions. I could no longer believe what was being taught by the Church. What was I to do? Where could I go to find answers, to find the truth? I cried out to God in prayer and asked God to speak to me directly. Since the only mention of God speaking to humans in the *Bible* was to the prophets, this was a drastic move on my part.

When the communication began during meditation, I wrote down everything I perceived in my mind. My normal thoughts were still there, but there was another set of thoughts, as if they were in my right brain, and my normal thoughts were still happening in my left brain. At first, of course, I thought I was schizophrenic; even though I had asked for the experience, I never really expected it to happen.

During the weeks that followed, I meditated daily, sometimes several times a day. In the original communications, I felt I was communicating with God or maybe Jesus, since this was my only reality. As the communications continued, one day I was introduced to several spiritual beings. The consciousness with which I spoke suggested these beings were other members of my Oversoul. This was a concept I had never heard of before. Spirit said some people would consider these beings their "guides," Angels, muses or daemons.

It was explained, the Source, or Creator God, had sparked off parts of itself into large soul consciousnesses, and through time, these large consciousnesses sparked off parts of themselves into the next lower dimension. Therefore, down through the dimensions between the Third dimension of Earth and the Source, each of us has other Oversoul aspects operating simultaneously in other dimensions. It was also pointed out that we had the ability, through altered states of consciousness, to communicate with these other aspects of our Oversoul family. This totally blew holes in the Christian doctrine I had lived by.

It was then suggested in the writing for me to research the work of a woman named Jane Roberts who had written several books with an aspect of her Oversoul called Seth. Reading these books and especially the novels she wrote about a being she called Oversoul Seven, not only made me more comfortable with the idea of the Oversoul, but also made me laugh. I highly recommend the Oversoul Seven series to you.

Having only the awareness in Christianity that the psychic or occult is to be avoided, I had no understanding of what it was to be psychic or the meaning of the word metaphysics. I went to the *Random House College Dictionary*.

"Psychic: Of or pertaining to the Human soul or mind; mental (as opposed to physical) outside of natural scientific knowledge; spiritual – a person who is sensitive to spiritual influences or forces."

I had seen psychics and fortunetellers around Jackson Square on a visit to New Orleans. I was sure I did not want to become an obese woman with gray hair, wearing long dangly earrings, sitting at a warped card table shuffling tarot cards. The very idea horrified me.

"Metaphysics: The branch of philosophy that speaks of first principles or the ultimate nature of existence, reality, and experience, especially as developed in self-contained conceptual systems or extending beyond the limits of the physical and psychological."

That sounded interesting and not so strange, and not what I had perceived "psychic" to be. Could there actually be a branch of philosophy I'd never heard of that related to this strange, multi-dimensional experience I was having?

I then decided to look up the words spirit, soul, medium and New Age.

"Spirit: The incorporeal part of a Human in general, or of an individual, or as an aspect of this, such as the mind or the soul."

"Soul: The spiritual part of a Human, regarded in its moral aspect, as capable of surviving death and subject to happiness or misery in a life to come. The principle of life, feeling thought, and action in Humans, regarded as a distinct entity separate from the body. The spiritual past of a Human as distinct from the physical part." (That sounded a lot like reincarnation to me.)

"Medium: A person serving, or conceived to be serving as an instrument through which another personality or supernatural agency manifests itself." (By that definition, I would have to define myself as becoming a medium. Yikes, I wasn't sure I wanted that title either!)

"New Age: The ending of the 2,000-year Age of Pisces and the beginning of the 2,000-year Age of Aquarius."

Then for some reason I felt compelled to look up Catholic.

"Catholic: Pertaining to the whole Christian body or church. Universal in extent, encompassing all; wide ranging." (This didn't sound like the definition of the Holy Catholic Church, as I knew it, but maybe this was the inference in the Episcopal prayer book, even though I had not understood it as such, nor had it been explained by the priest in that way or, for that matter, in any other way.)

I was told by my soul I could continue my education by reading the works of Ruth Montgomery who was a respected newspaper reporter. She had begun to have experiences of receiving information through writing from what she called "discarnate spirits."

Although her works did not include information specifically about the Oversoul, they did explain many other spiritual subjects I had wondered about. I highly recommend her books to you.

I will refer to the Oversoul as the various levels of ourselves that operate in other dimensions between God and us. When I see a person's Oversoul energetically, it looks like a giant fireworks display, with explosions or expulsions of energy being projected down or lowered from one vibration or dimension to the next lower dimension. When I first began to see the silver cord coming out of a person and flowing above them, I was intrigued enough to follow the cord, and when I reached the next dimension of that person, I saw a connection to other energies, entities. Following it further into the next dimension, the same thing happened. In each dimension, there would sometimes be one, but usually several beings connected to the being whose silver cord I was following. At a certain level, not always the same dimension, I would find the original entity that projected down the soul aspect into the current incarnation, or current soul aspect, experiencing life in the Third dimension.

We are projected into the Earth plane from a higher level of consciousness by a much larger consciousness. What is the purpose? It seems that in each incarnation the consciousness has the ability to expand and evolve, depending on the experiences of each lifetime and the awarenesses gained. The Oversoul oversees the life, but does not control it. Once we are incarnate, we come under the Universal Law of Freewill. We can choose to behave as we wish and to believe as we wish. We do, however, come with a purpose. The purpose is spelled out in the contract we make with the other members of our Oversoul before we agree to each incarnation. Once we wake up to this awareness, that there is a purpose to life, and ask for help to achieve that purpose from our soul, or Oversoul, or God, help will be given. The Oversoul, Angels and God are not allowed to intervene in our lives unless we ask; this is the purpose of prayer.

We previously existed in the Third dimension. Earth and Humanity are moving from the Third dimension toward the Fifth dimension. At the time of this writing, we are in the Fourth dimension, which Christians would consider to be hell. The Fourth dimension is also often referred to as the astral plane. The Fifth dimension would be considered by Christians as heaven. Around Earth, vibrationally, exist other dimensions. Beyond the Fourth dimension, the Spiritual Hierarchy of this Universe has set up an energetic barrier called the "ring pass not." The purpose of this energetic barrier is to keep the negative thought forms of Humanity and atomic repercussions from polluting or destroying the rest of the Universe. This ring of energy is periodically tightened causing time, as we know it, to speed up. As the Fourth dimension is moved toward the Earth by this tightening of the ring-pass-not belt, Humans will experience the results of all our previous thought forms needing to be transmuted or forgiven. We can do this by calling for the assistance of Saint Germain and the Violet Flame of Transmutation. Earth and Humans are evolving into the Fifth dimension. We are currently in the beginning of the Fourth dimension, which accounts for the amount of disease, anger, fear, addiction, hatred, violence, murder, rape, deception and craziness we see being acted out around us.

Souls whose bodies die when their energetic or etheric bodies are too weak to make it through the Ring Pass Not can become stuck in the astral plane or Fourth dimension. Christians would see this plane as hell. The reason they see it as a lake of fire would relate to the energies of the first three chakras, energies of survival, emotion and sexual energy, which would be seen as red, orange and yellow. If a person, during their life on Earth, is consumed only with thoughts of survival or sensory experiences, it is possible their energies would be too slow to make it possible for them to enter the Fifth dimension or higher; these dimensions would be referred to by Christians as heaven. Jesus is quoted as having said, "In my Father's house are many mansions." I believe He actually meant there are many other dimensions.

People who are addicted to a behavior or substance are usually feeding the addiction of several entities. The only way a "stuck" soul can feed its addiction, once it is out of the body, is by joining with (possessing) the body of someone who is practicing their drug or behavior of choice.

## PRAYER OF EXORCISM

Through the power vested in me by the Cosmic Christ Consciousness, I deliberately call forth the Arch Angel Michael and the Band of Mercy to enter this person, (use name) their home, place of work, their car and all places they frequent. (You can clear buildings and machines, etc. with this prayer.) I ask that they remove all negative energies and entities. I ask that these energies and entities be escorted into the light that they might continue to grow and prosper. I ask that this person be triple sealed from any future invasion by astral energies or negative thought forms. And so it is. (You may choose, or not, to tone audibly or internally to create a stream of light.) Kodoish, Kodoish, Kodoish, Adonai, Sabayoth (say three times)

In communicating with the other aspects of our Oversoul, we can bring more and more consciousness into our bodies. It is possible for a higher vibrational aspect of our Oversoul to over light our bodies to give a speech, create a piece of art, music or writing when invited. It is possible to establish such a strong connection with a higher level of one's Oversoul as to have constant contact. I recommend we strive for this communion. The purpose would be to learn why we are here in this particular incarnation and to make sure we fulfill that destiny. This level of our Oversoul also has the ability to become our guide, mentor, inspiration and receptionist with other souls and what I call our "gatekeeper." A gatekeeper is one who protects us from being approached by spirits who do not have our highest good in mind or who are not from our same Oversoul.

Often, in this dimension we will meet someone else who is projected from our same Oversoul. When we meet these individuals there will usually be instantaneous energetic reactions, which might feel either positive or negative. Since we do not have a category for understanding this intense reaction, it is not unusual for one to jump in bed with the person. Often, we will incarnate with other members of our Oversoul to accomplish a large group project. Since we most often incarnate with the same souls time after time, whether to balance past karma or to work on new projects, it is normal to meet other people who seem familiar to us. We might think of these beings as soul mates, kindred spirits, or other Oversoul aspects. Richard Bach's book *One* is useful in understanding more about the Oversoul, and also simultaneous existence.

The following is a diagram I made to help me to conceptualize the Oversoul:

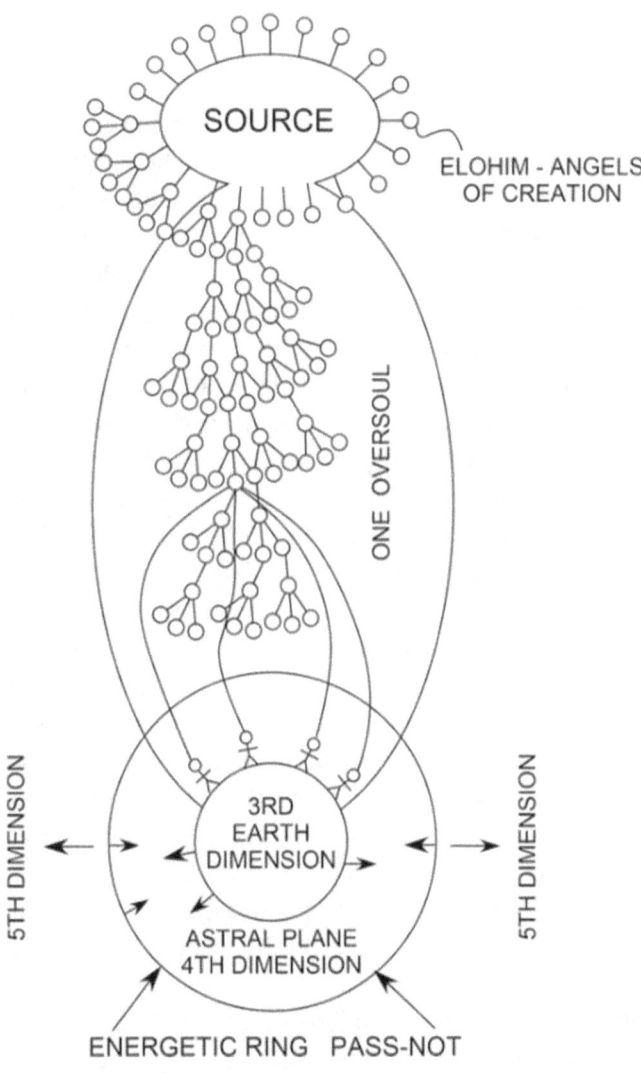

# 2.

# Consciously Opening to the Oversoul

When I first began opening to my Oversoul and hearing and seeing multidimensionality, I noticed a phenomenon which I did not understand. When I stared into someone's eyes, my perception would shift, as if I went through that person's eyes and up through the crown of their head while following an energy cord. The cord seemed to connect that individual to a series of energy fields and, ultimately, to a much larger energy mass. Eventually, the cord connected to what appeared to be the Source of all energies.

The energy fields resembled continually exploding roman candles, with descending spirals of energy forms coming from the Source energy toward the Earth. These spirals of energy moved out in all directions, connecting all the stars and planets. But let me describe this another way. When I look into a person's eyes and go energetically back to the Source, I see something that looks like a giant fireworks display, as if the Source sparked off energetic parts of itself and those parts are large enough to spark off parts of themselves and to bring down those "aspects" of themselves into lower vibrational frequencies for the purpose of experiencing life in these various dimensions. These "aspects" are all energetically connected. As far as I'm aware, there is no set number of members in one Oversoul.

Then, I began leaving my own body etherically through the crown of my head to explore my own soul's structure. Understanding began coming more fully, and eventually I connected with an "aspect" of my soul in the sixth dimension of consciousness. This soul aspect referred to itself as my "Source Self" and welcomed me to call it Matthew. I questioned Matthew about the descriptive terms he used.

He explained that "aspects," or "co-beings," are terms used to describe one unit of soul consciousness operating as a separate personality in a vehicle created of Light particles and infused with soul essence, sometimes physical.

"Soul Self" is the aspect of the soul choosing to send a portion of its consciousness into another Light body, or physical body, for an additional set of experiences.

Matthew further explained that the "Oversoul" refers to a group or family of souls (similar to a family tree) descended directly from the Source. I understood that if anyone could trace their true family tree far enough back, the person would encounter the <u>Source of everything</u>.

All souls are connected. However, there are levels of vibrations and planes of experience operating simultaneously, with <u>seemingly</u> separate existences. The separateness appears to be more realistic or pronounced between the physical and non-physical dimensions. This is because of the "veils" between the level of consciousness and the dimensions of vibrations.

Matthew's explanations were always precise and as simple as he could make them while clarifying such complex subjects. He also continued to explain that translating spiritual principles into English is very difficult because English is a language designed for commerce, not spiritual expression. However, he continued his explanation, saying, "co-beings" or "aspects" enjoy a shared memory and a shared sense of self at the level of the RNA/DNA memory. The soul memory, or dianetic memory, includes the pattern of experiences of the <u>entire</u> Oversoul, not just experiences of a single personality.

This explained to me that if I allowed myself to regress many, many times to past life experiences, I would begin to see a chronological overlap in what I experienced as linear time.

I understood that in order to create space in our cells, or DNA, it is wise to erase negative and traumatic memory patterns from the DNA. Various methods of DNA clearing are available from Namaste Enrichment Center. Radionics is one. "Circles of Life" processing is another. Still another method, which Matthew channeled to me, is given on the CD called the "Cellular Release of Fear, Judgment and Negativity."

My understanding of all of this information about the Oversoul is: when our system was created originally, the Source sparked off parts of itself and created the 24 Elohim, or Creator Spirits, usually referred to as The Builders of Form. These entities sparked off parts of themselves and created what are known as souls. They worked with certain extraterrestrial groups and Metatron to create the original Human matrix through the various stages of Human evolution from cave man to Cro-Magnon, to

Neanderthal, to Homo erectus, to Homo sapiens and now to Homo universalis. These powerful and creative beings sparked off energies which became souls or the higher aspects of Oversouls. The matrix for the Human containers, "bodies," has been upgraded through evolution and through extraterrestrial and spiritual influence through the centuries.

An Oversoul is a family whose members vibrate at a higher vibrational frequency (a non-physical frequency) than that of the Third dimension. I refer to the Oversoul's family members as "aspects" of the Oversoul. Each of us is a part of a more complex energy field, a member of an Oversoul. Aspects of our Oversouls experience life in other dimensions and in this dimension simultaneously. Some aspects are on other planets; some are a part of other star systems, or in inner-Earth civilizations; and some are aboard light ships or in other bodies here on the planet.

Oversouls project aspects (of themselves) into this Third dimension at different ages. Put another way, many of our Oversoul family members may be of different ages and sex than us. Other members (or aspects) of our same Oversoul family have a vested interest in communicating with us and in assisting us to accomplish the missions we came to Earth to do.

When an aspect (or member) of an Oversoul decides to incarnate on Earth to experience physicality, a contractual agreement is made: to wit, the aspect will work toward certain types of growth for the benefit of the entire Oversoul. Everything the incarnate aspect accomplishes spiritually assists the growth of every other aspect of the entire Oversoul. The agreement is in the incarnating aspect's superconscious and can be accessed or remembered by the personality-self through meditation and soul communication.

The part of the Oversoul agreeing to lower a portion of itself (an aspect) to become physical consults various expressions of the Oversoul and the Karmic Board (as part of the agreement). Considered, for example, are features and characteristics of the Oversoul family which could stand strengthening or increasing. Because of the Universal Law of Karma, the Law of Cause and Effect, energies must stay balanced to enable the Universe to function as intended.

When a member of an Oversoul is "aspected" into Earth's Third dimension, its contract or agreement spells out the race, sex, economic conditions, country, parents and certain "classes" it will take while on Earth, even the potential of how many bodies it will create for other members to inhabit. Classes may be such things as: Physical handicap, incest, alcoholic or drug-using parents, divorce of parents, being raised by a single parent, being adopted, etc. Further, an incarnating aspect sets up what I call certain destiny points or tests as part of the agreement. These tests are to happen at certain ages, and are for the purpose of determining spiritual growth. Tests may include happenings such as graduation, marriage, accidents, severe health challenges, divorce, and bankruptcy, death of a parent, child, spouse or close friend.

When the aspect or person reaches the destiny point, or age, the event happens. How a person responds or reacts to the event, and how severe it needs to be, is a gage by which spiritual understanding and growth can be measured. To illustrate, it is obvious that, at certain times in our life experience, a divorce would feel totally devastating; we could feel as if we had lost our entire identity, our entire reason for living. At another time, if we have spiritually progressed to understand who we truly are, we might be able to view it as both a release from karmic agreements and freedom to move on up the path toward a new and exciting future.

**Everything between destiny points is created by our day-to-day thoughts, be they positive or negative attitudes.**

This contract does not determine predestination; it only sets up possibilities. We always maintain our Freewill. I want to say here, again, that the Oversoul who "aspects" a part of itself into the Third dimension has an energetic investment in that aspect accomplishing its goals. The Oversoul **understands the difficulty of the assignments**. Remember, though, since evolution happens in accordance with the Divine Plan, the Plan has been in effect for a very long time.

Multi-dimensionally, various aspects of our Oversouls (and, therefore, of ourselves) are having many different types of experiences simultaneous to ours. Some of these aspects may be of the same or opposite sex as we us. Some will be androgynous, containing equal masculine and feminine energies. Some will be extraterrestrials. Some will be very much like ourselves, except operating in alternate realities, or what we think of in linear time as alternate pasts and futures. This is because all time is simultaneous in the space-time continuum.

If we were to accomplish regression, or progression, through hypnosis, we could possibly experience some of these simultaneous alternatives. Occasionally, we may glimpse them from the altered states of sleep or meditation. These aspects of our soul may serve in the roles of guides, teachers, mentors or protectors.

Human beings have the ability to communicate with these other aspects; i.e., to ask them for assistance and advice. However, because of the Universal Laws of Freewill and Non-Intervention, these soul aspects may ignore us, to a certain extent, <u>unless we seek out and specifically ask for their help</u>.

Matthew jokingly stated, *"When a Human being begins meditating and asking for assistance, it is as if a "blue light special light" begins pulsating above their heads. Oversouls watch and wait and hope for these lights to begin pulsating"*

Once we become acquainted with these other aspects of our Oversoul (of ourselves) we can consciously merge with their energies. Thereby, we can gain greater volumes of information, resources, spiritual knowledge and energies.

Some of our soul aspects will also be incarnate on the Earth plane when we are. Oftentimes, we are brought together with them for group interactions, projects and just to have emotional, physical, psychological and spiritual companions on our journey back to the Source.

We can usually recognize a soul aspect through a resonance of energy which feels totally comfortable and reassuring to us. And this familiar energetic reaction will happen whether the aspect of the Oversoul is in a physical body or spirit.

However, there is nothing to say that this will be a positive energetic reaction. These beings can be very clear mirrors to us of our unresolved issues. Feeling agitated by someone from your own Oversoul is possible too, because of past life experiences. While such beings can assist us with much soul growth, all may not be fun or without confrontation. This is why I do not advocate a person seek their soul mate or another member of their Oversoul as a mate; this is however, up to a person's personal choice. It is usually easier to be in a mated relationship with someone not of our same Oversoul.

Also, there are those Oversoul aspects that came to Earth before us, who became awake and aware during their Third-dimensional stay. They understood those of us who would come after them would need energetic assistance with their mission, especially during this critical period in the evolution of Earth and Humanity. They hermetically sealed a portion of their consciousness for a future Oversoul aspect to pick up. When we travel to such a location, the hermetic seal containing the consciousness is opened by the Universal Light Language symbols in our energy field.

For us to accomplish spiritual growth, it is helpful to work toward communication with the various levels of our Oversoul, through intuition and sometimes through telepathy. In some cases, when certain vibrations are reached within the body (and in accordance with some prior-to-incarnational agreement), other aspects of the Oversoul will join, braiding their energies into the consciousness of an aspect using one vehicle (or body). This is called "soul braiding." Usually, there is a subtle, but not dramatic, personality shift when this braiding occurs. The aspect that comes does not bring personality, only consciousness; but the expanding of consciousness will often cause changes in a person's personality. This process is often also referred to as "over lighting."

Several aspects of one Oversoul can braid themselves into one life stream and work through one body during the course of a lifetime. When more than one aspect braids into one body from the same Oversoul, this being is then referred to as a "composite". Many walk-ins later agree to become composites in order to have as much of the Oversoul energy as possible available in this dimension.

Soul braiding is not to be confused with a walk-in situation. In a walk-in situation, the original aspect returns to the Oversoul and leaves the body to another aspect. Neither of the instances of "soul braiding" nor "walking in" is possession. Possession is the unlawful overshadowing of one consciousness (or more) in a physical body by a consciousness from the astral plane. This is contrary to spiritual law. Soul-braiding and walking-in are in alignment with spiritual law, and the aspect walking-in is always from the same Oversoul.

Some individuals now on the Earth plane made prior-to-incarnation agreements to allow their vehicles (bodies) to be used by what is known as a "group mind." This kind of contract constitutes several Oversoul aspects "braiding" into one life stream, or "group energy" moving through the vehicle periodically, without braiding their consciousness permanently into the vehicle's personality for the purpose of teaching through the person or doing special forms of creativity through them.

When an aspect of the Oversoul dies or leaves the physical body, it may or may not rejoin the Oversoul immediately. There are options: (a) It can retain the personality and energies and reside near the Earth plane to assist others; (b) It can surrender its personality identity and rejoin the energy pool of the Oversoul; (c) It can retain its energy on the Earth without a body and wait to give its energy and consciousness to another of its Oversoul aspects; or (d) In the case of an Oversoul aspect(s) who came to Earth before us, it can leave its assigned energy and wisdom hermetically sealed in the Third dimension in the location of their physical death.

Regarding the hermetically sealed energy/wisdom, those of us who have come to Earth at this time come with Universal Language-of-Light symbols in our energy fields which make it possible for us to <u>merge</u> with the Oversoul's hermetically-sealed essences when we come in contact with a location where a previous conscious Oversoul member has hermetically sealed a portion of their consciousness to be retrieved at a later time by someone who can use the consciousness to serve the Earth and Humanity. Likewise, in the case of energies and consciousness waiting to be given to another, aspects (Humans on the Earth) will be drawn energetically to locations where previous entities resided so the merger can take place.

Oftentimes, the TRUE purpose of people's urgings to travel is to "soul merge" or "pick up" an extra energy or energy aspect of their Oversoul. This energy aspect may either be ready to leave the Earth life and willing to donate a portion of consciousness it has carried, or it may have already left its earthly life, in the physical sense, and left a portion of its consciousness hermetically sealed in this dimension.

If the aspect has already left physical life, as explained, it may be waiting energetically to give its energies and consciousness to one who will be committed to using this portion of soul energy for the benefit of the entire Oversoul.

Soul mergings are not something to fear. They are great gifts offered to us by our Oversouls. I recommend you follow you intuitive urges to travel. People may or may not be totally aware physically or consciously at the time they merge with other aspects of their Oversoul, but their consciousness and energy will expand. They don't have to do a ritual, or do anything, to cause it to happen. All that is required is that they (people) travel with **intention to merge with higher levels of themselves. Everything in this dimension is based on intention**.

Oftentimes, when such mergers take place, people (Human beings) are not conscious of what has happened. They may feel expanded, briefly disoriented, or sad or elated for a short time before continuing normal expanded awareness and energy. Some time may be needed for the physical body to adjust to the additional energies. If people are aware of such possibilities, they are advised to consciously request the merger take place with "no negative side effects and without resistance." They should also ask the Oversoul to transmute the energies before they (the energies) are merged with those of the people doing the merging. This is so the transmutation, after the merger, will not have to be done through the physical and emotional bodies of the ones doing the merging. They can ask that it be accomplished with ease and grace.

It is **very important** now for people to work through and only accept guidance from their own Oversouls. Seeking guides and teachers from one's Oversoul family ensures receiving the greatest amount of assistance and personal Truth. **It is important not to call in extraterrestrial forces or other spiritual teachers other than those of one's own Oversoul.**

For spiritual readers and healers, it is especially important, if you wish to call in guides (yours or those of the person you are reading for or healing) that you try doing it through contacting your own Oversoul first, and ask your Oversoul to contact the other person's guides from their Oversoul. I do this by mentally intentioning a beam of energy sent into my Oversoul, just as you would if you were plugging a cord into a switchboard. This is much less confusing and is easier for your body than operating empathically. It will also get you clearer, more complete information you can trust.

Here is an effective method you may use to contact your Oversoul: When you meditate, ground yourself by sending beams of energy from the soles of your feet into the core of Earth. Seal the room in which you are meditating from astral interference. Begin pulsating energy at the point of the mid-brain (the pituitary and pineal glands are located at the mid-brain) and open the crown chakra (top of your head). Through thought and intention, send a beam of energy from the mid-brain up through the corridor in the astral plane (or Fourth dimension) to the Fifth dimension of your Oversoul.

You may desire to ask your Oversoul for a name or identifying sound, symbol or vibration as recognition you are successfully making contact. Usually, the flood of love and or concern that overwhelms you is sufficient for you to "know" you have connected successfully, will be enough. While contact with the Oversoul may not always occur, I feel strongly it should be sought during meditation.

As our energy vibrations expand and increase, we are able to reach more and more aspects of the Oversoul in all dimensions, eventually reaching our I AM Presence, our Guardian Angel and the Source.

After your soul vibration and your body vibration synchronize, you will be able to consciously merge with each aspect and level of vibration, incorporating increased consciousness and access to the Oversoul's combined knowledge. When I first started working with Matthew in 1982, his vibration was of the Fifth dimension. Through the years, as we have both progressed, his energy and mine are now of the eighth dimension.

Many people deliberately avoid meditation and soul communication for fear of what they will hear, what will be expected of them, fear of change or of having to give up familiar or known lifestyles. Avoidance behavior is futile and makes life more difficult. The entire purpose of life and the incarnating process is to remember, to communicate and to accomplish the life's goal.

If we spend our lives in avoidance, the soul continually co-creates circumstances with us to promote growth and complications to encourage us to seek communication with God and to reach to the soul for help. If we procrastinate too long in avoidance, the soul, after many attempts to get our attention, withdraws its energies from the physical and personality self and the body dies.

The soul energy then returns to the Oversoul to evaluate its progress and to be reassigned by the Oversoul to another life and body to work out the same issues and learn the same lessons, similar to having to attend summer school.

Immediately upon leaving the body, a hologram of our life's events flows before us. As our own judges, we compare the events with the agenda, or agreement, for the life we made before incarnating. We can then see where "we missed the mark." In archery, this term is defined as "sin."

One of the reasons people fear death is, during the current lifetime, they shun or shy away from doing what they were scheduled to do for the Oversoul's benefit on the inner planes. Since we Humans are "dipped in the bath of forgetfulness" at the personality level before each incarnation, we do not remember our purpose, agreement or previous lifetimes **until we consciously seek to remember**. In each successive lifetime, we increase our awareness and knowledge. The more conscious each aspect of the soul becomes during each incarnation, the quicker memory of the soul is restored, and the stronger the Oversoul becomes, proportionally.

Many children are being born now (sometimes referred to as Star Children) with thin veils, or no veils at all, between their personality selves and their Oversoul selves. These children will be more difficult to control and confine and will have trouble conforming to our standard educational programs. This is because they remember Universal truth and will not accept dogma, convention or lies as a way of life.

## GROUP MINDS

Within the various levels of our Oversouls are what we could think of as "terminal mainframes" (using computer terminology). These "mainframes" house vast quantities of information.

In spiritual terms, these "mainframes" would be referred to as "group minds." The various "Brotherhoods," i.e., the Great White Brotherhood, the Brotherhood of the Rosy Cross, the Sisterhood of the Shield, the Order of Emerald Fire, the Order of Amber, the Order of the Golden Dawn, are names given to just such spiritual orders.

After Humans have done a certain level, or volume, of spiritual work, clearing negativity from consciousness, and have begun to communicate and follow the soul's guidance, they may receive an invitation to become an active conscious member of one, or several, "group minds."

These groups have various spiritual functions and focuses. Some are healing orders, some work with teaching, some with politics, some with economics, some with art, and some with music. Some work primarily with Human evolution, some with Earth evolution, and all with spiritual evolution. Being inducted into an Order is called Initiation.

Receiving this type of invitation denotes the spiritual student has reached a certain level of integrity, discipline and dedication. It is similar to a job promotion in a corporation, or receiving a "password" into a level of information to which we have not previously had access, or a key to the executive washroom. This type of access is not lightly offered to a spiritual student. Nor should the student accept it lightly. The more knowledge we receive, the more we are expected to share with others. The more we know, the more Spiritual Laws or principles we are expected to practice.

# 3.

# Meditation For Meeting Members of Your Oversoul

If you would like to meet members of your Oversoul, follow these instructions:

Sit at a desk or table where you will not be disturbed and compose yourself.

Seal the room you are in on the North, South, East, West, the ceiling and the floor from any negative influence or entity.

Ground yourself into the energy at the center of the Earth.

When you are completely relaxed physically and emotionally, and clear mentally, take three deep breaths, letting each one out quite slowly.

Deliberately open your heart to all levels of your Oversoul including the Ascended Master Octave of Light.

Take a deep breath, roll your eyes upward and hold the breath and count to yourself, 3,3,3 at the point of the midbrain to deliberately activate the pituitary and pineal glands, then exhale.

Take another deep breath, eyes upward, and hold it at the midbrain count 2,2,2, and exhale.

Take a third deep breath, eyes upward, hold it at the midbrain and count 1,1,1, and exhale.

Begin to count, descending slowly from 10 to 1.

You are now at a level of mind (the Alpha level) that makes it possible for you to separate your consciousness from your physical body to travel spiritually.

Intend and imagine a multidimensional elevator that looks like a regular elevator.

Stand in front of the elevator and expect the door to open.

When it opens, enter the elevator and the door will close. Ask your body intelligence to raise the vibration of your physical body to match the vibration of the Fifth dimension. Push the button in the elevator marked "5."

Wait for a few seconds while your body vibration changes and the elevator ascends to the Fifth dimension. The door will open.

Step out of the elevator and greet any being who has come to greet you.

They know who you are, so you can ask for their name and ask how they help or relate to you in your physical life.

Using your imagination, know what they look like. Look around you and determine if you are inside a structure or outside. Notice the air and the brightness of the light. Each dimension you enter will be larger and more open than the one before and the beings may be taller in each dimension. You may write down or record what you learn and what you observe. If you do not record the information in some way, it will be easy not to retain what you have observed and learned. Each time you enter a dimension, the person or persons who greet you may be different.

When you feel you have completed your communication with your Fifth dimensional self, thank the being for meeting you and mention you will visit them again. Enter the elevator again. The door will close. Ask your body intelligence to raise the vibration of your body to that of the next dimension. Push the button for only the next higher dimension. The elevator will ascend, as will your body vibration. When the elevator door opens, step out and greet the being or beings who are there to greet you. Ask for names and ask for how they have or can help you in the future. Pay attention to everything you can see in each dimension.

Take it slow. Do the meditation often and move only up one dimension at a time. Eventually you can meet many members of your Oversoul and this process can assist you to ascend your own vibration gradually.

We have the capacity, as Humans, to learn to connect and communicate with twelve levels of our Oversouls.

# 4.

# Rainbow Bridge to the Oversoul

Now is the greatest moment in the history of the awakening of the Human Spirit. We have more help and energy available to us than ever before. This energy is causing some people to have spontaneous Kundalini awakening. This can be very harmful to the body, emotions and psyche if we do not prepare ourselves for the awakening. In order to take advantage of this opportunity, it is important to deliberately build a bridge between your personality and your soul, Oversoul or your Higher Self. You can think of it as a bridge linking your conscious mind, your sub-conscious mind and your superconscious mind.

Building a rainbow bridge from the heart, through the pituitary and pineal, to the Oversoul is mandatory to a spiritual connection that is satisfying, healthy, useful and sane. Opening to spiritual energy and realms without this deliberate connection can cause confusion, emotional instability, physical health diminishment and insanity.

Ancient wisdom teachings call this connection the "antahkarana". It is the link between the personal and impersonal Self, the personality and the Higher Self. We shall refer to it as "the rainbow bridge".

The Higher Self reaches us through a soul sound within our hearts. Each soul sound is unique. Each thing that comes into physical manifestation actually occurs as a result of sound frequency.

A new and intense energy is spreading throughout the atmosphere of Earth. This energy is the energy of the Cosmic Christ Consciousness, the energy of the "messiah", avatar energy, or master energy. It will be experienced as an inner note. The sound is silent, inaudible to ordinary hearing, but quite clear as it vibrates within the center of the soul. This note is of a higher frequency of Light than has here-to-fore been available to Humanity in the past and comes as a response to our prayers and desires for peace. As this energy hits the planet, it shakes up all that is not of the higher vibration. The degree to which people hold onto those things that are not of the higher vibration is the degree to which they will experience pain. This energy is available to anyone who is prepared to tune in to it and to use it for the greater good of all concerned. It is time to develop the ability to receive messages accurately from our Higher Self and to live from the authority of our Higher Self instead of the expectations of others or our ego.

**We teach best by making our own life work through manifesting what we need and desire in order to express our true self and demonstrate the joy and abundance available by the authority of our Higher Self.**

Each person will receive information differently. Some people will feel it, some see it, and some hear it. It has been my experience, once I agreed to "know" and not to demand to see, hear or have physical proof, that the information became stronger and more complete. I recommend you agree with your soul to accept and expect "to know".

We can begin this process of building the bridge through intention and commitment. Each time you meditate, ask for a thread of Light to be added to your connecting bridge; ask for an additional soul quality to be manifest in your life. With each thread the bridge will become stronger.

Soul qualities you might desire to ask for are:

| | | |
|---|---|---|
| Wisdom | Oneness | Knowingness |
| Love | Patience | |
| Truth | Acceptance | |
| Trust | Perseverance | |
| Courage | Higher organization | |
| Joy | Vision of the future | |
| Confidence | Peace | |
| Humor | Enthusiasm | |
| Beauty | Serenity | |
| Harmony | Understanding | |
| Compassion | Heart Connection | |

When you have your bridge in place you can use it for many things.

If you have a person with whom you are having trouble communicating Third-dimensionally, you can meet them on your rainbow bridge while they are sleeping and have the conversation with them there. Later, when you encounter them, the communication may seem to them as if it has already happened, or they will understand your desires better. Many things can be resolved in this way. You may also take your manifestation desires onto the rainbow bridge and release them to the Universe to be fulfilled through divine right action.

One technique that has served me well through the years is what I call projecting myself into the future. If a person calls or writes to me and asks me to be somewhere, or to participate in something, I deliberately mentally project myself into that setting to see if I am there. If I can't find myself in the setting, I know I am to say no. If I've planned an outing or a trip, but begin to have doubts about it, I do the same thing. Sometimes you will strongly believe you are to do something, and then as the time grows closer it may no longer by advised by the soul as the best use of your energy.

We have what I call possible futures and probable futures. Every choice we make changes the possibility of our future. One path is lit up by the soul at a time; this path is the probable future. If we are a person following our intuition to deliberately be in the flow, we will find ourselves living in the probable future. If we have certain habits we like, or refuse to change, these habits will lead us into a possible future; this future however may not be the future the soul had in mind and it will be more difficult. There is a difference in following habit and following intuition.

## EVERY CRISIS OPENS THE SPACE FOR A RICHER LIFE

Each crisis reflects some area of life that is being healed or awakened. Of course, these are easier to see in hindsight. Ask that your insights come quickly. Often the loss of money or a job, even the loss of a relationship, offers a level of freedom, self-awareness and identity that was not there before. It is possible it will create a space for a much more fulfilling life than what was lost.

Try using everything as a metaphor. When I pull weeds, I have an intention of pulling out and throwing away old beliefs from my sub-conscious that no longer supports the life I desire. When I throw something away, or give it away, I feel space opening around me and within me. When I finally get around to doing filing, I feel my thoughts coming into more order. When I water the flowers, I give thanks for the beauty around me and know it is reflected within me through my intention. When I dust, which is one of my least favorite things to do, I feel the cobwebs clearing out of my mind and feel my thinking become clearer.

## WHAT'S NORMAL

As we awaken spiritually, we sometimes question our own sanity, and certainly those around us often question our sanity. If people around us have radically different beliefs than we do, it is easy to question your right to your beliefs. We question: Is it sane to be in the majority or to be in the minority? How can we convince our partners and family we are not going off the deep end with our radical new beliefs? How can we convince them that our minds are still sound and convince ourselves that we are not going too far out? We **do not** have a responsibility to convince them. We do have a responsibility to check out our thoughts and ourselves with our souls. The process of enlightenment requires a well-integrated personality base for the Higher Self's guidance to work through.

We are on the leading edge of a new consciousness. We are no longer a part of the majority. Any knowledge that goes beyond popular beliefs can sometimes make you feel isolated, especially when there is no proof in the outer World and your friends have not had similar experiences. It is important not to attempt to convince anyone else to energetically or philosophically come with us. The soul's journey is a solitary journey; everyone should take the trip when they are ready and at any speed they choose. It is comforting to have people to talk with about our experiences, but it is important to choose these people wisely. Don't try to impress or convince anyone of your spiritual maturity level. Spiritual inferiority and superiority are both inappropriate. If you are living your life from your own spiritual direction, your quality of life will speak for itself. Then if others come and ask you questions, if you are connected to your soul, you will have the words you are supposed to say that will not be confrontational.

Intention is the most important quality we can have when working deliberately with our soul. Don't ask for knowledge of the future; ask, "What is the next single thing for me to do or know now for me to be in a state of divine grace?" The answers will come in knowingness.

## A PROBLEM CANNOT BE SOLVED
## AT THE VIBRATIONAL LEVEL IT WAS CREATED

In order to actually solve or resolve a problem we've created for ourselves, we need to go to a higher vibrational level for the solution. This solution can occur to us from our intuition, our sub-conscious, .and our superconscious, or in a dream. When we have a problem to solve, we can take it into meditation or ask our soul for a solution while we are sleeping. It sometimes helps to do a ritual to jog the assistance we need, such as drinking half a glass of water before going to bed, with intention to receive the answer to your dilemma from your soul. Put the glass beside the bed, and upon awakening, drink the other half of glass of water with the intention the solution to your question will be given to you within twenty-four hours. If we do not wait for an intuitive answer to our problem, but proceed to "fix" the problem from our intellect, we usually create at least three additional problems. The problem is "patched" to reoccur again in another form. If we ask for answers, we must figure out intellectually how to use the answers. If we wait for the intuitive <u>solution,</u> the problem can be resolved in a way that causes us to get the lesson and <u>dissolve</u> the situation in such a way that it will usually not reoccur. I suggest asking your soul for solutions rather than answers or fixes.

# 5.

# The Oversoul and Channeling

I've been taught by my soul that each of us has an Oversoul family, a group of souls who operate together to learn and express certain lessons and talents. It is sometimes referred to as simultaneous lives in various dimensions. At some point, an aspect develops enough consciousness and energy that they are able to project a portion of themselves into the Third dimension to experience life for a very specific purpose. In order to determine that purpose, it seems only logical it would behoove us to communicate with that part of our Oversoul that projected us into this dimension. In my opinion, that is the appropriate reason to desire to channel and the logical reason to channel our own Oversoul rather than to just open to channel any spirit that makes itself available to us. Through communication with your Oversoul, you can then communicate with any Spirit or group mind your soul deems necessary. You can have access to Universal Intelligence. I recommend you establish a relationship with the highest level of your Oversoul, through the Cosmic Christ Consciousness, that your physical body can tolerate. This entity will then, through invitation, become your "gatekeeper or receptionist" within your Oversoul. This keeps you from being bombarded by every entity that wants to try to speak to and through you. Your gatekeeper can then limit who approaches you and filter information that is not accurate or to your highest good. It also makes it possible for you to trust what you receive from your Oversoul.

There are several kinds of channeling: trance channeling, conscious channeling and automatic or inspired writing. These are the three types I would like to discuss. To trance channel, a person must go into an altered state of consciousness, losing awareness of their body and their surroundings to allow a disembodied entity (a Spirit without a physical body) access to their body and vocal cords. The person agreeing to be the conduit through which the information will come is usually referred to as the channel or the medium.

When I personally began to channel, I had never heard the term "channeling" nor did I know anything at a conscious level about metaphysics or mediumship. In 1979, I went through a series of death experiences: my mother's death, my father's remarriage, a divorce, leaving my community and family to move to another city, only to have my fiancé die of a heart attack four days after I arrived to be married, and the relinquishment of my children to be raised by their father while I regained control of my emotions. I was excommunicated from the Episcopal Church by phone by the Bishop of West Texas and the Bishop of Oklahoma for letting a priest who I wasn't married to die in my bed.

I turned inward and repeatedly asked God, "Why me? What have I done wrong?" I kept asking for answers. None seemed to come. One day I went to a bookstore to seek a book on the subject of finding my life's purpose. "Why am I alive?" I kept asking myself. While I was in the bookstore, a book entitled *Psychic Energy* by Joseph Weed fell off the shelf in front of me. I had never heard of metaphysics and what I had heard about psychics was all negative and nebulous. I denied the book and returned it to the shelf and went to the Psychology, Self-help and Religion section but found no book on how to find your life's purpose. As I was leaving the store, I again passed the Occult section of the bookstore, and now the book was surrounded by a white moving light. You can imagine how confused I was and amazed. I was sure I was having a nervous breakdown. I had never seen this type of phenomenon before. My curiosity or "something" encouraged me to buy the book, which I did.

I took the book home and said a prayer to God, "If you have a message for me in this book, please put it on one page and I will open the book to that page, read it and expect a message." The page I opened to, gave instructions for meditation to receive inspired or automatic writing. I had never consciously meditated. The article said, "Prayer is talking to God, meditation is listening to God." More than anything else, I desired to hear God. I desired to know what God desired me to do. I desired to know why I had experienced so many difficulties. Out of frustration and desire to know, I fearfully tried the meditation in the book.

The first time I tried the meditation, I did everything exactly as suggested. I took a shower to symbolically clear my aura, even though I didn't know at that time what an aura was. I took the phone off the hook.

I lit a white candle and sat up straight on the couch in a loose-fitting robe, with bare feet on the floor, pencil and paper on my lap. As I did the breathing and counting as it was described in the book, I experienced an argument going on inside my head. The words from my left brain were, "This is not going to work; this is the dumbest thing you have ever done; for God's sake, put the phone on the hook and go get a job." On the right side of my brain were other words, "Through this pen will come the words you need." This was repeated three times when I didn't begin to write. I am not a very patient person so after three repetitions I yelled, "What?" I then realized I was to write what was being telepathically inserted into my mind. The message impressed on the right side encouraged me to keep trying the meditation. After only a few minutes, the encouraging voice overshadowed the discouraging one and began to speak to me of who I really am and why I am here.

I did not receive the information in automatic writing; I received the information in inspired writing. During automatic writing, another entity takes control of your hand and actually writes the message for you. During inspired writing, the words or images are telepathically imparted into your brain and you write the impressions you receive in your mind in your own handwriting. Actually, the information is given as blocks of energy and your brain creates words to explain the energy.

As I stated previously, I had never heard of channeling, automatic writing, inspired writing or metaphysics. My first thought was that I had become schizophrenic, because there were two trains of thought; not two voices, but two trains of thought. I was concerned I had, through all these traumatic experiences, split into two personalities. My first messages included the suggestion I try this method of communication for thirty days before making a judgment or giving up. I knew that piece of advice wasn't coming from my conscious mind because I am not a patient person and would not set myself up to do anything for thirty days. I continued the process daily, sometimes three times a day. The information proved valid and gave me a great deal of hope. I was eventually led to other people who were having similar experiences who could verify I was not crazy, but had, through my desire to know, tapped into communication with my Higher Self, or my Oversoul. You can imagine how relieved I was to find I was sane; not only sane, but on my way to knowing, understanding and working out why I am on the Earth.

My experience did not happen in automatic writing, nor do I recommend automatic writing or trance channeling to you. <u>I do not advocate giving up</u>

control of your body to any other entity. I do advocate learning to channel your own Higher Self, Oversoul or God Self through meditation, conscious voice channeling or inspired writing. I advocate learning to channel your own Higher Self in order to learn why you are here and how to most effortlessly get on with doing what you came to do. I also recommend it as a way of knowing how to stay healthy. Your Higher Self can tell you what your body needs nutritionally.

The first questions I always ask students are: "Why do you desire to channel? Who do you desire to talk to? What do you desire to find out? What are you going to do with what you learn? Are you willing to talk to just anyone in order to have the experience? Are you willing to discipline yourself to keep your body healthy with the additional energy you will receive? Are you willing to do physical exercise to stay grounded, strengthen the cells of your body by taking mineral supplements if necessary, get regular amounts of sleep, drink eight glasses of water per day?" If they are not sure, I ask them to think about it for a week and get back to me later.

I find a lot of people want to play around with the idea, which is why they have been drawn to play with Ouija boards or automatic writing. They are not serious. I am here to tell you that playing around with spiritual practices and channeling when you aren't serious can be a very dangerous thing, dangerous for you physically, emotionally, mentally and spiritually. If you are not serious, do not begin, do not open up. It is far easier to open up than it is to shut down.

Many of our mental institutions are full of people who are possessed as a result of opening up to astral influences without proper guidance. The astral plane refers to the plane occupied by the recent dead and non-Human Nature Spirits, or "Elementals." Many people open up prematurely through the use of drugs and alcohol. Some people actually split their consciousness into more than one dimension and find it difficult to reconnect themselves. The astral plane is full of beings that have died in a state of addiction to drugs, alcohol, food, sex, power, money and/or control. Once out of their bodies, they are stuck with their addiction and have no way to act it out or fulfill it without entering another physical body. Therefore, it is very easy to become possessed. Suggested reading on this subject: *The Unquiet Dead* by Dr. Edith Fiore, or *When Rabbit Howls* by Trudy Chase. Dr. Fiore believes that eighty-five percent of the patients who come to her for psychotherapy are possessed with from one to fifty additional entities.

Ouija boards have been around for a very long time and have a lot of lower-vibrational astral energy attached to them. I do not recommend playing with a Ouija board for any reason. A person will normally attract very low vibrational entities by communicating through a Ouija board, especially if they are not trained to seal the room they are in against any negative energies or entities through prayers and invoking only entities of your own Oversoul. Challenge any entity that shows up in your meditation by demanding, "Are you from my own Oversoul?" If the entity is not from your Oversoul, break the connection.

Ouija board communication can become addictive or compulsive. People allow themselves to be fascinated by the energy moving the planchette, the information they receive and the unknown origin of the movement, energy and information. Entities can attach themselves to your aura or your physical body, or take up residence in your home after being invited by you to speak through a Ouija board. I had a very traumatic experience during my early period of psychic work. I warn you, from my own personal experience, not to use a Ouija board from my own personal experience. If you feel this has happened to you, break the Ouija board into at least three pieces and burn it to deliberately disconnect yourself from the Spirits you contacted through the board. After burning it, ask to be strongly reconnected only to your own Oversoul.

## JUST BECAUSE IT'S CHANNELED, DOESN'T MAKE IT TRUTH!

Students find when they first start coming to my class that various fears begin to surface: fear they will be taken over by some outside energy, fear of the abuse of the power they will gain by their ability to channel, fear that communication with their soul will require them to change their habits or lifestyle, fear they will be asked to give up certain relationships, their job, or place of residence, or the unknown, fear of what the soul might ask them to do. My fear was that I would be asked to go to Africa to be a missionary. Some fears actually come through from other lifetimes when we have been active channels and have experienced persecution and even death for the use or abuse of this gift. It is a gift, a talent, which can be developed or received from your soul. Most past life fears can be eliminated through energy transfers or hypnosis. Other fears must be overridden by your desire to know being stronger than your desire to stay the same.

It is very important to clear all of your energy bodies before you open to channel. You have four energy bodies and an etheric field of thought around you that all hold thought forms. We hold fears, some of which have been projected to us from others and some we brought forward from other lifetimes, and all are collected in our auric field. If we do not clear ourselves, we will not bring through accurate information. It would be like making coffee for years with the same filter and wondering why it did not taste good. If you are mentally or emotionally confused, the confusion will be amplified and intensified by the additional energies coming into the body. Fear is not necessary if you become educated before you begin and use the precautions you learn.

You are a spiritual being, a spark of energy, or a soul sent out from an Oversoul to inhabit a physical body. That Oversoul wishes to communicate with you. It has waited your entire life for you to remember, to acknowledge its existence and to ask for help. You have aspects of yourself operating in various dimensions, simultaneously.

The beings in the first level of the soul, from the Source, are what I refer to as the Angels of Creation; we each have an Angelic Presence. We are aspects of much higher-level beings that chose to send a portion of their consciousness into Human form. That is why my soul says we are aspects, of and from, a higher frequency vibrational being that "aspected" us into Human form in the Third dimension. The My Soul calls us "units" of energy. I prefer the word "aspects." Before you left the Oversoul, you had a conference with the Soul and signed a pre-natal agreement to do certain things for the Soul to clear a part of the Soul's karma. Karma is a negative effect of the misuse of the Universal Law of Cause and Effect.

You may have agreed to create certain things, learn certain lessons, teach certain principles to raise the consciousness of Earth, or maybe to create a certain number of vehicles for other souls to inhabit, i.e., to have children.

If you agreed to have children, you also agreed to be responsible for them for a given period of time. This period of time is not arbitrarily eighteen years or twenty-one years. In some cases it is a very few years. In other cases it may be many years. If you try to be totally responsible for these souls, children, beyond the length of time you agreed, you hamper their spiritual growth.

You also set up certain destiny points in this agreement. We set up these destiny points to check our progress, or to make sure we have opportunities for certain lessons. First, we choose to be either male or female. We choose the nationality and area of the World where we will be born. We choose our parents. Destiny points are usually events such as marriages, divorces, bankruptcies, graduations, when or if to have children, abortions, accidents, education, career changes and certain trips, or relocations. How we respond to these events when they do occur in our life will let us know the level of our spiritual maturity, how well we have learned our spiritual lessons. All events between these destiny points and, in fact, the points themselves, are controlled by our thoughts. We also plan in include what spirit calls "windows of opportunity to leave" the life. Often, we leave ourselves more than one time frame from which to possibly exit the body.

You may also have other aspects of your Oversoul incarnate in the Third dimension and you may meet them. It is not necessary to know this at a conscious level, but you will have an energetic reaction when you meet another individual from your same Oversoul. These individuals would also be known as soul mates, kindred spirits or soul aspects. They will not necessarily be of the same sex or age group as you. You may ask your soul if a person you know or meet is from your same Oversoul.

Because of the Law of Freewill, which is a gift of God, your Oversoul is not allowed to interfere in your life unless you ask. Negative Spirits, lost Spirits, Spirits who are dead and in the astral plane and do not acknowledge that they are dead, do not honor this law. I recommend opening only to channel your own Oversoul. If you find, after you have opened to your soul, that you agreed prior to incarnation to be a public channel, or to be a spiritual counselor, your soul will teach you or lead you to someone who can teach you to perform what I refer to as a "conference call" between your Higher Self and the Higher Self of your client or audience to receive the necessary information. It is also very important to learn to move through dimensions of the soul and reference only one dimension at a time. There are many different levels and dimensions of the soul.

If you open to your soul and ask for energy or information and do not return energy to the soul through toning, song, creativity or prayer, you create unbalanced karma. If you pray and do not receive what you ask for, you can be sure it is untimely or karmically incorrect. The soul always listens; however, it sometimes seems to not answer. Karma is a negative effect resulting from misuse of the Universal Law of Cause and Effect. Without these Universal or Spiritual Laws, the Universe would be in chaos. These Laws exist and operate whether we are conscious of them or not. Spirits exist whether we acknowledge them or not. Previously, the Karmic Board met only twice a year on December 31st and June 21st of each year. Now, to assist in lightening the density of humanity's accumulated karma, they remain available 24/7 for us to approach them with requests to balance certain karmic situations. We now have the right and authority to ask the Karmic

Board to balance our own karma, the karma of our family, the Earth, and to dissolve the karmic residue left by wars, terrorism and cataclysmic events.

If you are going to channel, I suggest you begin by saying: "I deliberately call upon the energies of the Archangel Michael and the Band of Mercy (a group of Angels who are committed to clearing the Earth of negativity and evil) to remove any negative influences, entities or energies from this room and my body. I request this room to be deliberately sealed on the North, South, East and West against any negative energies or entities. I seal the ceiling and the floor. (There are energies which are not entities.) I deliberately open myself as a channel for the power of the Holy Spirit and the Cosmic Christ Consciousness level of my own Oversoul."

If at any time you feel agitation, it is good to reuse this invocation. It also works as a Prayer of Exorcism. You have the ability to exorcise a person or place, but it is a better and safer plan to use the intercession of the Archangel Michael and the Band of Mercy. Never get into a confrontation with a spirit. When you discharge a being or negative energy, it is a good idea to replace the space with Light by toning. Whatever tones come through you, intuitively, will be correct.

Toning is a very powerful tool. Each soul has a vibrational sound. I recommend you practice toning intuitively to locate your own personal vibration. When in doubt use the tone of Aum (pronounced OM).

We are in the Fourth dimension, which is full of souls who died violently and were not prepared for death; many are not aware they are dead. They are looking for ways to express themselves. They are looking for bodies to attach themselves to, people who are using the drug or behavior of choice they were using at the time of their death. They are in "hell" with the addiction still present in their body, and their only relief comes when they vicariously feed off the body of another using their same addiction. We have the power to assist these beings into the Light through the use of this same prayer. It is important to clear the astral plane of these wayward entities. **Use the grounding process and exorcism as previously described.**

## MEDITATION

If you are grounded, say something similar to: "I invite the Presence of my Oversoul, Master Guides, Teachers and Angels to be present and receptive to me. I open myself as a channel for the power of the Holy Spirit. I ask that only the highest and purest form of truth be allowed to come through me. I ask for access to the Akashic Record. I ask to receive only that which is to my highest good." (Or the highest good of your client.) If you are reading for someone else, connect from your Oversoul to their Oversoul to receive information for your client from the client's Oversoul, and not their energy field, thought forms or emotions.

Begin to be aware of your breath; breathing from your abdomen, allow your breath to become even, the same length of inhale as exhale. Totally relax your body with your spine straight and your bare feet on the floor. Take a deep breath, holding that breathe at the point of the mid-brain as you count to yourself silently, three, three, three, and exhale. Take another deep breath, hold it at the point of the mid-brain and count to yourself silently two, two, two, and exhale. Taking a third deep breath, holding it at the point of the mid-brain, repeat to yourself silently, one, one, one. Continuing to breathe normally, allowing your body to become more and more deeply relaxed, count backward slowly, silently, ten, nine, eight, seven, six, five, four, three, two, one. Mentally intend to go to a beautiful quiet setting which may be out-of-doors, a temple or a room of your own mental creation. Wait there in a meditative state to receive messages or images. It is good to keep a pencil and paper on your lap to record the images or words, or you may prefer to use a recording device.

Say a prayer of thanksgiving after you have received a message or inspiration or at the end of your meditation, even if you feel you did not receive that which you desired. It may take several attempts before conscious contact is accomplished. The goal is to reach the alpha brain wave level and to stay there during the meditation without dropping into theta or delta. Alpha is where the communication is possible.

If you open to channel large amounts of creative energy and then do not use this energy to create, it can have a negative effect on your physical and emotional body and potentially cause depression.

***If you become spiritually aware and then decide you are so evolved you do not need protection or clearing, you are using a similar logic to learning how to drive a sports car and believing you are immune to accidents, so you do not put on a seat belt and drive recklessly.***

If you pray about an issue and do not listen for an answer of what you are to do actively to cause the miracle, you are not behaving in a spiritually mature manner. Prayer cannot be left to a minister or a priest; it is a personal matter between you and your soul.

It is very important to learn to channel responsibly, with integrity and in a manner that is healthy for your body. Part of your integrity needs to include not tuning in to other people's minds, emotions and soul records indiscriminately, out of curiosity and without their permission. It is important to overcome being empathic, which is against spiritual law.

You need to be a person of integrity if you are going to accept the responsibility of channeling for other people. It is spiritually incorrect for us to enter the Akashic Record for a client. When you connect your soul to the client's soul, you can include asking for access to the Akashic Record in your opening prayer. Then if it is relevant to that person's situation, the information will come from their soul, through your soul to you, to be revealed. If you are a channel and wake up one morning emotionally or physically distressed, it is important **not** to open to channel for your clients, and to reschedule their appointments. You need to decide on your own principles. Will you channel information about the sex of an unborn child, will you tell someone if you see they are approaching death or an accident, or that a loved one is approaching death, that one of their children appears to be on drugs or is having sexual relationships? It is ultimately important to be tactful but honest. Most things can be worded in such a way as to be alluded to, but not blatantly explained, to put a question in the client's mind that they may, themselves, question or explore the answers. Everyone has possible futures depending on their choices. The soul will point out the probable future the client will have if they continue as they currently are thinking and feeling. We all have access to our own answers within ourselves. We are sometimes too emotionally distraught or unclear or too lazy to seek these answers, and then need a channel we can trust.

When you first begin to channel, your body may sway, move slightly in circles or shake as the energy begins to move through the body and the body adjusts to it. Once your blockages are removed, the swaying and shaking normally cease. Some people experience tears when connecting to higher energies if their emotional bodies have been damaged.

Once you have opened and asked to talk with your Oversoul, they will send you messages in many ways: TV, radio, music, other people, clouds, symbols, animals, books, magazines and newspapers. When you notice something becoming repetitious in your life, take it seriously. If a word or idea comes several times in a week, research it in the library, on-line or from other sources. You have a responsibility to be active and not to expect everything you need to know will be given to you directly by words in your head. The information is downloaded in an energetic form; your mind and body will then transmit the information to your conscious mind in words, ideas, pictures or feelings.

You may also choose to explore Tarot cards, astrology, numerology, runes, crystals and other methods of divination in addition to direct channeling to receive information. Many individuals use these kinds of tools to open to their soul. If you are open and receptive, you could do a runes reading, a tarot reading, or meditate to receive inspired writing, and all three should essentially tell you the same or similar information.

Develop discernment; ask your soul for the gift of discernment. Discernment is the most practical of all the spiritual gifts; it allows you to know when someone is telling you the truth, or a thing you read or hear is the truth. Discernment differentiates between truth and illusion.

It is possible to channel on the phone for another person because we each have a unique individual voice vibration which is reflective of our soul and is as unique as our fingerprints.

Our ultimate objective in coming to Earth was to remember the possibility of this connection to the soul, seek it, allow it and benefit from it. In allowing more and more connection to the soul aspect that sent us, we can allow this aspect to over light our bodies to become "soul-infused personalities." We can allow this communication with soul to happen at all times, not just when we are meditating. To begin to allow the connection during meditation is the first step; the second is to allow it during our sleep state, and then to allow it during our constant waking state. Once we have agreed to this soul infusion, our intuition will increase and we will be virtually channeling our lives as they were intended from the level of the soul. In this state, life is more effortless, more enjoyable and more rewarding both for us and for the soul. Always be cautious, but not fearful, because fear attracts negativity and attracts that which you fear. Use knowledge to overcome fear.

Intend and agree to live in a state of soul awareness, self-awareness. Being aware of how we "feel" at all times is a clue to soul awareness. Negative feelings are a warning sign from the soul that we are out of balance or off track of our goal, the soul's goal through us. Become aware of your heart's desires, because your heart's desires are your soul's desires. We came here to enjoy the process of being Human and to enjoy the beauty and variety of all that is available on the Earth. We can do that most successfully by channeling our own Oversouls.

# 6.

# What Reincarnation is and How it Works

We all spring from the same spiritual Source. We are one Human family that has been incarnating together for Ages. We will be working together in many cycles to come. If we were to recognize this fact and act accordingly, peace would rein on Earth.

Each of us is an aspect of divinity, projected to Earth by our Oversoul for a specific reason, with a specific mission, and to balance a portion of the accumulated karma of our Oversoul family. When we come to Earth, we are assigned to a specific family of our choosing for the purpose of having the perfect circumstances to learn the lessons desired by the soul, and to repay the debts of, or to accept the benefits of, previous karma. We have within our cells the memory of all lives lived by all members of our Oversoul. Because of this, if we regressed hundreds of people, which I did in the 1980's, we would find several people who believed they were all the same famous figure, such as Mary Magdalene, Napoleon, Queen Victoria, the Apostles John, Mark, Luke, Matthew, etc. At first, this was very confusing to me and I felt the regressions could not be true, even though I was experiencing the reality of the events with the clients. Once the idea of cellular memory information was explained to me by my soul, it made more sense. Karma is not just individual. It can be collective to a race, family, Oversoul and nation. This is why, from one life to the next, we might agree or decide to be born into different races, religions or sexes.

The one who exercises the right of choice prior to incarnation is not the previous personality, with its likes and dislikes, but the indwelling permanent individuality, the soul. Its choice is not based on personal preferences, but on needs, the need to become a totally balanced Human being, with all its powers and faculties harmoniously developed. Jesus,

Buddha, and Krishna all embody both male and female qualities. Dynamic strength and power are equally blended with gentleness, tenderness, and compassion; wisdom with humility; extraordinary abilities as leaders and reformers with patience, persistence, and endurance.

The answer to the current imbalances in the World cannot be resolved by more and more women assimilating themselves more and more into a literally man-made World, but together balanced, women and men creating a new future.

If, in a previous life, we were a part of a nation that fought a war against another nation because of religious beliefs, we will logically create our next life in the system or belief we fought against, or destroyed people for believing in that religion. It is our soul's desire to experience all possibilities of Earth life for the benefit of learning. The sooner we learn how to operate within the Universal Laws of Earth, the sooner we can have lives that are not about struggle and existence, but are about abundance, grace and service to the Earth and Humanity. I have written a book for the Spiritual Hierarchy a book called The Universal Laws and Jesus' Meaning of the Beatitudes which is now available on Amazon.

We are not here today and gone tomorrow through death to live eternally in some heaven or hell. We are consciousness that is, by our own choice, recycled into Human experience to continue the cycle of creativity. The sooner we understand the system and agree to participate from a conscious perspective, the sooner we can remember why we are here and get on with our mission in a way that is fun, less stressful and productive.

At the level of the soul, the consciousness is neither masculine nor feminine. At the time of making a particular incarnational contract, we decide which type of body would most accommodate the lessons we are attempting to learn through this particular incarnation. Sometimes when incarnations are very close together, and little time is spent out of body in the Oversoul, the residue of the previous life very much flavors the experience of the next life. A person who has been male and chooses his next life as a female may still feel like a man trapped in the body of a woman and vice versa. When one sex dominates another, he or she may incarnate next time in that very sex, not as a punishment, but as a learning experience.

This may be easily true if the person has committed suicide in the previous life. When a person commits suicide, it is imperative that they reincarnate quickly to finish the contract of the life they sought to escape, plus take on an additional contract that is usually more complex and challenging than the one they chose to leave prematurely. Only on rare occasions does a person come in with a contract in which they give themselves permission to commit suicide at a given time.

A speedy reincarnation can sometimes result in a birthmark where a previous wound was experienced in the most recent previous life, or a weakness in that part of the body. The wound to the etheric body does not have time to heal or be corrected if a person reincarnates quickly.

Intermissions between incarnations were once quite lengthy, as much as a thousand years, but are now shorter and shorter. Many souls realize the opportunity now present on Earth to make great strides in spiritual growth in one incarnation. Because Earth and Humanity are evolving into Fifth-dimensional essences, and we are at the end of an Age, opportunities are enormous. The Law of Karma ruled the Piscean Age and it was acceptable to accumulate karma and carry it over from one lifetime to the next. In the Aquarian Age, this will not be allowed. Karma will become more instantaneous. The Laws of Harmony, Grace, Balance and Beauty rule the Aquarian Age. Now that we have entered the Aquarian Age, it is imperative we clear up and balance our previous karma. This makes it possible to understand why so much is happening so quickly on Earth and in our lives. Our current lives often feel as if we have lived several lives in one incarnation. Many people are married several times, or have several partners. Many people change careers several times and change the area of the country in which they live. Family dynamics are different. We have stepfamilies everywhere. This causes many diverse types of relationship possibilities and the challenge for forgiveness is available to us daily. If we recognize what is happening, we can be more gentle with ourselves and more conscious about why it is necessary to have so many different types of relationships within one lifetime.

We are technically operating in two bookkeeping systems at once. We are making entries in the system within which we are living, while simultaneously attempting to balance, or reap the benefits of, entries we or someone in our Oversoul has made in previous lives. People have jokingly defined karma as "double-entry bookkeeping on a celestial level." This record is called the "Akashic Record." Edgar Cayce said: "Akasha" is a Sanskrit word that refers to the fundamental etheric substance of the universe, electro-spiritual in composition. Upon this "Akasha" there remains impressed an indelible record of every sound, light, movement, or thought since the beginning of the manifest universe. The "Akasha" registers impressions like a sensitive plate, and can almost be regarded as a huge candid camera of the cosmos. The ability to read these vibratory records lies within each of us, dependent upon the sensitivity of our system, and consists of attuning to the proper degree of consciousness, much like tuning a radio to the proper wavelength. The Akashic Records are sometimes referred to as "The Universal Memory of Nature" or "The Book of Life."

There are four kinds of karma: boomerang karma, organismic karma, soul karma and symbolic karma. An example of boomerang karma is that of a person who had been born totally blind. In looking in their Akashic Record, their soul might reveal to us that they had previously lived as a member of a barbaric tribe whose custom was to blind its enemies with red-hot irons, and it was, the now-blind-person's assignment to do the blinding.

Organismic karma involves the misuse of the organism in one life with an appropriate affliction in a succeeding life. A man suffering from digestive weakness since infancy might have been a glutton in a previous life. As a person suffering from a heart weakness, he may have lived a life of being emotionally callous in the previous life.

Symbolic karma can be explained best by examples. A person, who in another life "turned deaf ears" to pleas for help, could be born deaf in their next life. (Deafness in other cases could have other causes.) An individual suffering extreme feelings of inferiority in this life, owing to smallness of stature, might have, in another life, been haughty, acted superior or condescending toward others, "looked down" on others or used their superior physique to take advantage of others. Of course, this is not the only reason a person might be born short.

All life is one, meaning Humans, plants, animals, minerals, water, air and ether. Every atom and molecule is connected and made from the same substance. We cannot harm any substance without causing karma for our race, our nation, our soul and ourselves. Animals have group souls which are administered by a group of Angelic beings called Devas. These Devic Beings create and maintain each species.

Consciousness evolves through the mineral, plant and animal kingdoms. Animals, Angels and Humans are of separate linage and do not cross-incarnate, nor do animals incarnate as Humans. It is possible for the consciousness of one animal to incarnate into another more evolved species, or for one breed of dog or cat to choose its next incarnation as another breed of dog or cat. We can help other species to evolve. It is important when we have a pet to be attuned to the Deva of that specific breed and to the individual consciousness of the animal. This makes it possible for us to assist that animal to accomplish its incarnational mission. When the body of an animal is failing it will often ask its owner to assist it to get out of its body so it can easily reincarnate as a newborn. The animal soul returns to the group soul, but may choose to actualize again as an individualized expression of the same species. It is usually about six weeks between incarnations for animals and they often return to the same masters to support that individual or family. We have the ability to assist an animal to evolve by teaching or training it. We have the ability to learn to mentally communicate with plants, animals and minerals. The more open we are to plant, animal and mineral communication the richer our lives will be. The more cross species communication we can accomplish as Humans the more we can assist in our own evolvement and the evolvement of the plant, animal and mineral consciousness.

An awareness of reincarnation can increase our adaptability to circumstances. If we consider karma and that our present existence is only a portion of a long journey, we can look at life from a more overall perspective. We can look at everything as temporary.

There is no proof of the survival of the soul, there is only evidence; each person must decide for himself or herself. Not unlike other Universal Laws, the Laws of continued existence do not depend on our belief.

If you wish to regress yourself or another person, you may choose to use the following process. This is not a process of hypnosis. At all times suggest that the client observe the life rather than to participate or feel the emotions of the previous life. If at any point they become emotional, ask them to back away from the scene or to remove themselves from the emotional body of the person they were then and to observe.

If you are regressing another, make the person comfortable. Have the person remove their shoes and lie down. Clasp the person's legs, one at a time, just above the knee and manipulate your hands downward, stopping at the knee briefly to make certain the knee is relaxed; then rubbing on, down to the ankle and bend the ankle; then massage the foot, and then the toes briefly and vigorously. Repeat this manipulation quickly. Next, place the palm of your hand on the person's forehead, and with little pressure, move the skin of the forehead up and down and sideways for a few seconds. This relaxation process should not be overdone.

If you are regressing yourself, begin at this point.

Ask the person to close their eyes and, after a brief moment, ask them to become a few inches taller by allowing themselves to stretch out through the bottoms of their feet. Then say to them, "Tell me as soon as you have done this." When they say they have accomplished this, pause a few seconds and say, "Go back to normal size. Tell me as soon as you have done this."

Then ask them to repeat the exercise, only the second time ask them to become "a foot" taller. "Tell me as soon as you have done this." When they agree, pause again and tell them to go back to normal size. "Tell me as soon as you have done this." Repeat the foot-tall routine again. Each time, ask them to tell you when they have accomplished the exercise.

Now, ask them to go to the other end of their body. "Become a few inches taller by extending yourself out through the top of your head. Tell me when you have done this." Then back to normal size. Then, do a foot taller three times through the head. Always ask them to tell you when they are done.

The next step requires another exercise. "Now, this time extend yourself through the head, face, body, arms, legs and feet. (Say this slowly, with a moment's pause between parts of the body.) In other words, blow yourself up just like a balloon. Tell me as soon as you have done this." Then go back to normal size. All of the time, throughout these exercises, be jovial and keep your voice firm and convincing, yet be ready to laugh, and keep the person going quickly and smoothly through these preliminary exercises. Once a person has done them well, there is never a need to repeat them.

Next, tell them to blow up like a balloon again, only much larger this time. When they tell you they have done this, ask them to go quickly and stand in front of the building where they live. "Tell me when you are there." As soon as they say so, start them talking. Ask them to see this and that, and to describe what they see. Tell them to look for, one at a time, the door, doorknob, windows, walkways, trees, shrubs, marks of any kind. After they see and describe to you, these objects to you, tell them to, "Go quickly and stand on the roof of the building and look down onto the road (or yard) in front. Tell me as soon as you are there." Ask them to see and describe such objects as trees, cars, a road, etc. When this is completed, tell them to go about 500 feet up into the air and look down. (One in a hundred may object at this point, but remind them quickly that they are still safe and in the room.) Then repeat the request. "Tell me as soon as you are there." Ask them to see what they can observe and report it to you; keep the person talking.

The person may tell you throughout this phase of outdoor work that they are "imagining things," but remind them gently that this is an exercise in awareness and continue as if they had said nothing.

After they have described to you things they see from this advantage of altitude, ask them whether it is daytime or nighttime. When they tell you it is one or the other, ask them to tell you why they think so. They will say something like, "It is daytime because everything is light and I can see just as if it were daylight, so it must be daytime." Or "It is night because I see streetlights and house lights," etc. Or, "It is sort of twilight, you know, just like after the sun has gone down." If it is nighttime or twilight in their vision, ask them to make it daytime – bright as sunlight. "Tell me as soon as you have done this." Then ask them to tell you why they think it is daytime. Keep the person talking, talking all of the time. If it was daytime to begin with, ask them to make it night; and then ask them why they think it is night. Then turn the day into night and back again at least three times, but be certain you finish this phase by having it daytime – a very bright sunny day.

Then quickly ask the person, "Who is making it night and day?" Most will quickly answer, "I am!" If they hesitate more than ten seconds, ask them, "Are YOU making it night and day?" They will agree. It is important they understand they are causing this change.

"Now, are you still high in the air?" The answer will be, "Yes." "Please keep the scene very bright. Come back to Earth in another lifetime you lived many years ago, the lifetime that will be most helpful for you to see at this time. Come down quickly as you go back in time; bring your feet down quickly and firmly, but gently, and stand on the ground. Tell me as soon as you are there."

Watch the person's face. As soon as there is eye movement under the lids, tell them, "Please look down at your feet and tell me what you are wearing on your feet."

The person will now be experiencing a good vision of a previous life. <u>They may feel, however, that they are making it up</u>. Assure them everything is fine and to just report what they see and hear.

Remind them frequently to, "Look out through your eyes and listen through your ears." Ask, "What are you wearing on the lower part of your body?" Wait for descriptions, but keep the person talking. The more they talk the better they will begin to see during the beginning regressions. Insist they do only what you tell them to do and answer your questions, remembering to keep the questions in some semblance of chronological order. Move the person onward in time – skip a day, a week, a month or year in their lifetime, but keep them moving and talking.

**THIS IS VERY IMPORTANT. At the end of viewing each lifetime, run energy through the person's body to heal anything from that**

**lifetime that needs to be healed and ask the soul to bring forward in consciousness any talents or love from that lifetime into this present time. Then ask the person to go to an earlier lifetime by requesting, "Come down in an earlier lifetime – look down at your feet and tell me what you are wearing on them."**

At the end of the second or third lifetime you have run them through, ask them to "die" and follow through the "death," asking. "What happens next?" No matter what they report, do not question the validity. This is new material for people to understand. After you have regressed a few people through several lifetimes, you will understand that this material is valid. When the person has run incidents between lives, ask them to find their present parents before they were born. This ensures they know they chose their parents.

Ask questions, questions, questions to keep the session moving. People have a tendency to want to be quiet and just observe, or to linger in one situation. This is not productive.

At any time during the regression you can ask the person, "Do you see any need to continue at this time?" Let them decide when to stop. You can also regress yourself or another person to a time period in this life for which you, or they, do not have clear memories.

When you regress this person at another time, make them comfortable (but there is no need to rub the legs), tell them to turn the lights on inside, and go quickly back to where they left off during the last regression. After three or four sessions, people should be ready to regress themselves.

I offer you this process, because I know it works. You use it at your own risk.

**Remember to energetically clear each lifetime, before you proceed to the next.**

# 7.

# History of Reincarnation

Some of the synonyms used for reincarnation in ancient writings may sound unfamiliar to us. In Western tradition, metempsychosis, Palin genesis, preexistence, transmigration, and rebirth are terms that have been used. Transmigration is a word that has been frequently misused to suggest the rebirth of Humans into animal forms. Many cultures believe in the evolution of matter from mineral to plant to animal and then to Human, but do not believe that once matter evolves to the Human stage, it can devolve to a lower form. In the Orient, the frequently used expressions for reincarnation are *punar-janman* and *samsara*, to represent the round of births and deaths.

Reincarnation is the teaching that each individual soul experiences many lives on this Earth plane, or on some other planet progressing through a field of matter. Each incarnation, into a new physical form and a new personality, is assumed by the soul, each adapted to the new opportunities for further growth and development it seeks. One of the important conclusions of science is that the sum total of matter and energy in the Universe is constant. Would not a consistent Universe preserve its highest manifestation, even as it preserves its lowest manifestation, matter?

The history of the Human race is built upon the rise and fall of highly advanced civilizations. A nation is born, gives rise to an expanding culture and civilization, ascends to great heights and then gradually declines or destroys itself with its advanced technology if that technology is not combined with advanced soul consciousness. The Universe, and therefore Humans, operate in cycles. These cycles, both Human and cosmic, are always spirals, similar but not the same, never returning to a former level. These cyclical catastrophes of civilizations have meaning and are never final. Everything evolves - planets, star systems, Universes, plants, animals, minerals and Humans.

Advanced souls incarnate as a group into a nation, bringing with them their enlightenment, teachings, and culture. Under their leadership, a nation flourishes, expands and rises to great wealth and influence. Then the original teachings, corrupted by less enlightened followers, lead the nation to destruction. A nation will only remain supreme as long as the people choose leaders of integrity whose intentions are spiritual, political and economic freedom for the individual. If the masses elect leaders who are people of deceit who seek greater glory for themselves rather than for the nation, the nation will become weak because spirituality is forfeited for material power. When the civilization fails, the advanced souls incarnate in another nation and repeat the pattern. One civilization falls and another arises.

Inequality manifests everywhere in the World. Some people are poor, some are rich. Some suffer with manifold diseases, some are unexplainably healthy; some are deformed, others are beautiful; some are geniuses, and others are morons. God is just. He/She/It does not favor one creation over another.

Humans come forth in a variety of expressions: the bushman of Australia, the Eskimo of North America, the Wall Street tycoon, the yogi of India. What accounts for so many different types? Why have we come to Earth, this tiny planet revolving in the midst of space? We are not freakish accidents of time, space and molecules. We have purpose and destiny. God did not make these decisions, we did. God cannot rightly be blamed. We come each time to learn, to further our spiritual education through struggle to understand and experience the ALL.

Rebirth is an intelligent explanation of the inequalities of life. Each person is the sum total of his or her past actions and experiences in evolution. We are not the victims of a capricious God. Reincarnation is the most reasonable Law by which a God of Love could operate His Universe with justice and wisdom. Without a thorough understanding of reincarnation, life can appear utterly futile. There is little purpose for the struggle we put ourselves through on Earth, unless the experiences are for learning more lessons, developing soul powers to arrive at ultimate perfection, and through that perfection, attain union with God. Immortality is a word which stands for the stability or permanence of the soul.

> **"If immortality be untrue, it matters little whether anything else be true or not." H. T. Buckle**

The Egyptian Benu bird, the Egyptian phoenix, is traditionally used as the symbol for reincarnation. The bird is consumed by flames and arises from the ashes, once again whole. The Egyptians are the first culture to have obviously believed in reincarnation. Included in the Egyptian mysteries was the great Hermetic tradition. "Hermetic" means airtight or pertaining to alchemy or occultism (not disclosed, or kept secret). It also refers to the teachings handed down by Thoth-Hermes, which were often referred to as the teachings of Hermes Trismegistus. The Egyptians called Hermes by the name Tahuti, "thrice great", and the Greek equivalent being Trismegistus. Hermes Trismegistus was also a generic name used by various Greek writers on philosophy and alchemy. Hermes is the reputed author of the *Egyptian Book of the Dead*.

The *Vedas* are the ancient writings of the Hindu faith, they are said to have been written down by Lake Manasarovara in Tibet before the Hindus or Aryas descended onto the Indian peninsula from their original home in central Asia. The Vedas contain references to reincarnation.

The *Upanishads* are viewed as philosophic interpretations of the *Vedas*, and with *Bhagavad-Gita* they are considered the Hindu bible. The *Bhagavad-Gita* forms a small but important part of the *Mahabharata*. *Gita* means "song". *Bhagavad* is one of the titles of Krishna, one of the great spiritual teachers of the Hindus. His instructions are recorded in the poem. The teaching is of reincarnation. Gandhi's first acquaintance with this poem and the *Bible* was when he was in London to study law. He was introduced to the *Gita* by some Theosophists. Theosophists believe in a transcendent reality, which can be perceived or experienced mystically. Gandhi started learning about his own religion by reading the *Bhagavad Gita* and it became the most important book of his life.

The *Gita* appears, at first glance, to be about warfare, but Gandhi said: "I regard Duryodhana and his party as the lower impulses...Krishna is the Dweller within, ever whispering to a pure heart...An eternal battle is going on between the two camps, and the poet-seer vividly describes it. These interpretative clues make it possible to understand Arjuna's harrowing description (in the first chapter) of his confused mental and emotional state at the prospect of slaying his 'kindred'. Once any Arjuna, the hero in each Human, has resolved to live a higher life, his old selfish tendencies, or 'relatives', fighting for their very existence, throw up clouds of doubt, fear, and despondency to attempt to deter him from proceeding further."

Philosophically viewed, the three chief gods of the Hindus are Brahma, Vishnu, and Shiva, and are considered the Creator, Preserver, and the Destroyer. They are not considered to be anthropomorphic deities dwelling in their respective heavens, but beneficent, universal, impersonal powers at the root of all life, and which all beings are using all the time. Shiva, the Destroyer, is held to be higher than Vishnu because, in phoenix-fire manner, he destroys only to regenerate on a higher plane. All centers of life, from atoms up to worlds and galaxies, are therefore said to go through these cyclic periods of creation, preservation, and destruction, followed by regeneration or rebirth. Reincarnation is thus regarded as a Universal Law applicable at all times and at all levels of being.

After the *Gita's* translation from Sanskrit into English, it was read by Emerson, Thoreau and the group that later became known as the Transcendentalists.

**"As long as you are not aware of the continual Law of Die and Be Again, you are merely a vague guest on a dark Earth." Goethe**

In the Vedanta and Hindu teachings generally, previous existence and the eternal existence of individual souls is taken for granted, as it seems to be in certain passages in the New Testament (St. John 9). It is said, not by works nor by knowledge, but only through awaking to the oneness of one's true Self with the Eternal, does liberation come. Since the Self is witness of the body, its character, its acts, its states, therefore the Self must be of some other nature than the body. We are admonished to put away the thought that this body is the Self and to discern the universal Self, the Eternal, changeless self, and thereby enjoy supreme peace.

In India, the Hindu does not know the feeling of sinfulness. The word "sin" appears often in their religious literature, but the meaning to which it corresponds is different from the Christian definition. To them, every action entails, according to the law of Karma, its natural and inevitable consequence.

They believe everyone must bear those consequences for themselves; no merciful Providence can remove them. The Christian consciousness of sin depends upon the commandment to bear it in mind constantly, and this is what the Indian doctrine of salvation forbids. It teaches: as a Human thinks, so will they become. If a Human thinks of themselves constantly as bad and low, they will become bad. The person who does not believe in themself is considered to be an atheist in the real sense of the word. The highest ideal would be if a Human could think of themselves continuously, not as the most sinful of sinners, but as perfect. Such a Human would no doubt attain perfection even in this life. The Christian doctrine even identifies with the idea that we are born with original sin, a thought form totally foreign to other philosophies.

Hindus are not necessarily more spiritual than Westerners, but Karma and reincarnation are to them more than a dogma; they are like the air that they breathe. Hindus feel they are part of a cosmic scheme that is perpetually reviving itself.

Buddhism does not see itself, not as the record of the sayings of one man who lived in Northern India about 500 B.C. Numerous "Buddha's" appear and have appeared successively at suitable intervals of history. Buddha is not the name of a person, but designates a type. "Buddha" is Sanskrit for someone who is "fully enlightened" about the nature and meaning of life. The Buddha state is one of highest possible perfection and, it is assumed, takes many lifetimes and incarnations to attain this perfection. The most recent Buddha, Gautama (sometimes spelled Gotama) Buddha evolved from his position as a prince, who had been spared seeing anything that was not beautiful and healthy, to walking in the World to see all that Humans are capable of suffering. He developed a life and teaching of the "middle way," to move away from suffering toward enlightenment. The Buddha, standing on the threshold of Nirvana, took the vow never to make the irrevocable crossing so long as there was a single undelivered being on Earth. A similar pledge is traditionally ascribed to the Chinese Buddhist goddess Kwan Yin (sometimes spelled Quan Yin). Gautama Buddha now serves within the Spiritual Hierarchy as one of the Lords of Earth with Lord Maitreya and Lady Kwan Yin Buddha.

The Buddhist teaching found its way to Syria, Egypt, Judea, and Greece, and the groups like the Pythagoreans in Greece and the Essenes in Judea welcomed the new-old faith. Jesus, we know, was closely associated with the Essenes, and scholars now wonder about a possible Buddhist influence in the Sermon on the Mount, especially its love-thy-enemy theme so contrary to the eye-for-an-eye code of retaliation prevalent in his day and advocated in the Old Testament.

The Essenes taught the soul's pre-existence and held the Kabbalah in high esteem, therefore were obvious believers in reincarnation. The Kabbalists affirm that Adam was reincarnated as David, and is still to return as the Messiah.

The New Testament was not recorded until long after Jesus died, and its books subsequently passed through the censoring hands of church councils. In the sixth and later centuries when the present *Bible* was decided on, a number of differing gospels existed. Those deemed unacceptable were destroyed. By this time there was a strong anti-reincarnation sentiment in the Church and it would be surprising if anything on reincarnation managed to survive.

Jeremiah 1:4-5 says this prophet existed before his birth. "Then the word of the Lord came unto me (Jeremiah) saying, before I formed thee in the belly I knew thee; and before thou camest forth out of the womb I sanctified thee, and I ordained thee a prophet unto the nations."

It was generally accepted among the Jews that the prophets would return.

In Matthew 16:13-14, Jesus asked his disciples: "Who do men say that I the Son of man am? And they said, Some say thou art John the Baptist (who had already been beheaded); some, Elijah; and others, Jeremiah, or one of the prophets." In chapter 17:9-13, the disciples remind Jesus the scribes have prophesied that before the Messiah appears, Elijah, who lived centuries before, would come again and restore all things. Jesus replies that Elijah has already come. The disciples understood that he spoke of John the Baptist.

Jesus often spoke of his own previous eternal existence. "Ye shall see the Son of man ascend up where he was before." (John 6:62) "I am the living bread which came down from Heaven." (John 6:51)

Jesus was taunted by the Israelites for setting himself up as greater than Abraham. He replied: "Your father Abraham rejoiced to see my day; and he saw it, and was glad." Then said the Jews unto him: "Thou art not yet fifty years old, and hast thou seen Abraham?" Jesus said unto them: "Verily, verily, I say unto you. Before Abraham was, I AM". (John 8:56-59)

John the Baptist said of Jesus: "This was He of whom I spake. He that cometh after me is preferred before me: for he was before me." (John 1:14-15)

"Glorify thou me with thine own self with the glory which I had with thee before the World was". (John 17:5)

To the orthodox, Christ and Jesus are synonymous terms. Not so for the Gnostics and the Theosophists. To them, Jesus represented the personal name of their Teacher, while Christ is the divine Spirit in every Human. In a divine incarnation like Jesus and the Buddha, the Spirit was fully manifest. To the Gnostics, the words in Matthew 14:6, "I am the way and the truth and the life; no one cometh unto the Father, but by me," are words that have prevented many Christians from impartially investigating other religions. In this sense, the way would refer not to Jesus, the man, but to the Christ-Self, which is of the nature of "the kingdom of Heaven within you," of which Jesus spoke.

Saint Paul appears to use the word Christ in the Gnostic sense when he says, "I travail in birth again until Christ be formed in you" (Galatians 4:19).

Jesus continually referred to himself as the Son of man, not the Son of God. When the Jews accused him of setting himself up as God, he replied: "Is it not written in your Law...ye are gods?" (John 10:34) Jesus did not think of us as miserable sinners. When the disciples marveled at his so-called miracles, he told them: "Even greater things than these can you do also."

The Gnostics, Cathars, Jews, American Indians, anyone who believed in reincarnation was slaughtered by the Church. Why was the belief in reincarnation so offensive to the defenders of the faith, the Roman Catholic Church fathers? The believer in reincarnation tends to hold himself responsible for his own progress and salvation. Such a person has no need for priests and little regard for the literal dogma of the established church. The dogma (such as confessional) of redemption, conferred by institutional authority, was to believers in evolution through rebirth fraudulent or false. This accounted for their persecution and slaughter over many centuries while dogmatic religion remained in power.

There is no danger for a Muslim being called a heretic if he believes and expresses himself in favor of reincarnation; however, reincarnation is not taught to the masses because a subject like reincarnation demands a subtle mental attitude. It entails understanding of so many other teachings. Reincarnation was confined to the study and attention of the outer and inner students of Sufism. It was among the Sufis – from Sophia, wisdom – that the teaching of reincarnation was especially preserved. The Sufis claimed to possess the esoteric philosophy of Islam and to have preceded Mohammed by several thousand years. The eastern school of Sufis was derived from certain ancient Zoroastrian mystics. The Sufi doctrine involved the grand idea of one universal creed which could be secretly held under any profession of outward faith. Sufis believe in conscious evolution and the limitless perfectibility of Humans. Rumi was the greatest of the Persian Sufi mystical poets. His Mathnawi is considered next in rank to the Koran. The Koran, the bible of Islam, even though it has an esoteric foundation, is largely ethical in character.

The door that was shut by the Anathemas against preexistence in A.D. 553, and later by the extermination of the Cathars, Albigenses, Gnostics, and Knights Templar, was reopened prior to the Renaissance when Platonic philosophy was reborn.

Plato, Pythagoras, Socrates, Aristotle, Cicero, Julius Caesar, Vergil, Ovid, Plutarch, Emperor Julian, Proclus, Origen, Plotinus, Empedocles, Fludd, Dante, Leonardo Da Vinci, Shakespeare, John Donne, Chevalier Ramsey, Sir Thomas Browne, John Milton, Henry More, Spinoza, Leibniz, Voltaire, David Hume, Rousseau, Haydn, Mozart, Beethoven, Schubert, Wagner, Bach, William Blake, Napoleon Bonaparte, Wadsworth, Sir Walter Scott, Percy Bysshe Shelley, Bronson and Louisa May Alcott, Balzac, Victor Hugo, George Sand, Goethe, Benjamin Franklin, Henry Fielding, Immanuel Kant, Lessing, Glanvill, Hebel, Richard Wilhelm, Albert Schweitrzer, Leslie Weatherhead, Emerson, Longfellow, Whittier, Thoreau, Walt Whitman, Edgar Allan Poe, Oliver Wendell Holmes, Alfred Lord Tennyson, Charles Dickens, Robert Browning, Kierkegaard, Herman Melville, Dostoevsky, Tolstoy, Gauguin, George Bernard Shaw, Sir Arthur Conan Doyle, Henry Ford, Rudyard Kipling, William Butler Yeats, James Joyce, Sir Winston Churchill, Mainer Maria Rilke, Robert Frost, Jack London, Edgar Cayce, Hermann Hesse, Kahil Gibran, D. H. Lawrence, T. S. Eliot, Eugene O'Neill, Henry Miller, Pearl S. Buck, Aldous Huxley, Thomas Wolfe, Charles Lindbergh, J. D. Salenger, James Jones, Norman Mailer, to name a few, all believed in reincarnation. Many of them became Theosophists as a result of exposure to the writings of Helena Blavatsky in the Secret Doctrine and Isis Unveiled.

# 8.

# Reincarnation From A Personal Perspective

At the point in my spiritual progression when my Oversoul was mentioning past lives and simultaneous lives, I found these very confusing in light of my Christian perception of reality.

Through a series of synchronistic encounters, I met a man we shall call Joseph. I had a positive, unexplainably strong reaction to this man. I was puzzled by my reaction to him, since he was overweight, blond and fair-skinned, all things that would not appeal to me in choosing a mate. He treated me as if I didn't exist as a female, which I also found strange. At this point, Spirit suggested I experience a past life regression in order to cause me to believe I had lived before and would live again. I called the psychologist that was suggested in my meditation and asked if he did past life regressions. "Yes, occasionally," was his reply. I asked about the price of the session and he indicated it would be seventy-five dollars.

"Do you take credit cards?" I asked.

"No, but if paying is a problem, I do sometimes barter. What do you do?" he asked.

"I paint and do calligraphy," I offered.

"Well, I can't use those services, but I have been interested in trying a new technique I have with an artist to prove we can improve a person's creative abilities through hypnosis. If you are willing to come for four sessions of hypnosis for creativity and write up the results, I'll trade that for doing a regression for you," he offered.

I could hardly believe his offer. It sounded as if I were the one gaining all the benefits. I agreed, made the appointment and thanked him profusely. When I arrived at the psychologist's office later in the week, I was very nervous and unsure of myself. Dr. Ben is a huge, but soft-spoken, gentle man, who gained my confidence immediately.

## THE METHOD HE USED

I lay on his couch and he led me through a relaxation meditation.

"Four, three, two, one, you have now entered a state of deep relaxation. Your body feels heavy. You will begin to see colors, images…" The psychologist's voice was smooth, relaxed, reassuring. During the first session of regression I saw myself as a black slave who was raped and beaten to death. I came out of the regression exhausted and depressed. The psychologist assured me that subsequent sessions were unlikely to be as difficult, and that I might want to consider that the reason I had seen this particular life was to let me know the price one might pay for being in servitude to another.

Since I had no intention of ever marrying again or working in the corporate world, I felt I had eliminated the possibilities of being in servitude in this life. However, that week before my next session, Spirit began to suggest it would serve the soul for me to marry Joseph. I was distraught by the idea, especially since he did not seem attracted to me at all. The next regression gave me insight.

"Four, three, two, one, you have entered a state of deep relaxation. Your body feels heavy. You will begin to see colors, images." I floated through a purple cloud, then a yellow mist, and settled into yet another female form, more petite and fragile than the one my soul inhabits in this lifetime. Tightness in my chest let me know I was anxious, afraid. My hand smoothed the horsehair cushion of the train seat, my first train trip from Baltimore, leaving a family of ten headed only by my mother, no father image. I felt cast out, rejected, sold to the highest bidder.

The brakes of the train screeched and the steam hissed as the train ground to a halt. Chills ran up and down my spine as I braced myself against the seat. I was apprehensive about meeting this man I had been sold to by my mother as a mail-order bride.

My feet felt as if they were made of lead as I made my way down the corridor with my one bag, which contained my total life's belongings. My eyes searched the platform. I feared he was not there to pick me up and I feared that he was. My dreams of the past month, since I learned of my plight, had been filled with rape scenes of abuse at the hands of some faceless man whose hands violated my body.

As I saw this tall, broad-shouldered, round-faced, bearded stranger with happy, twinkling eyes approach the train exit, I stiffened. His voice, tentative, masculine and yet melodious, asked, "Becky?" I could only muster a nod. My voice escaped me, and my mind was wandering frantically in search of words to express my relief.

He took my bag and my hand, and gently guided me to a wooden wagon hitched to a beautiful bay horse. His huge, reddened hands encircled my waist and hoisted me into the wagon as if I were as light as a feather, but as fragile as an egg. Gently he placed me with respect in a position of equal importance on the seat, then climbed up beside me and took the reins masterfully and with authority. I observed, even in my fright, he did not slap the horse with the reins, but made a gentle clucking sound with his tongue against the roof of his mouth, and the animal moved forward with knowing, understanding his task. The giant of a man then turned his full attention to observing my face, my hands and my hair. While he said very little, he communicated warmth through his eyes I had never before experienced. His eyes seemed to hold some hidden message that I felt I would soon understand.

After two hours of travel through beautiful green rolling hills, we rounded a bend in the road and I saw a small log cabin nestled in the trees and heard the sound of a nearby brook as I sat in the stillness of the wagon.

Again, he lifted me effortlessly to the ground and took my hand to lead me to the stream. He motioned for me to sit on a rock that protruded over the water. After removing his boots and entering the water, he gently unlaced my high-topped boots and put my stocking-clad feet into the water, as if to ask me to remove my stockings would be premature, too familiar. His massive hands gently massaged my tiny aching feet, which had been encased for three days without the release for air. I was filled with awe, confused by my expectation in comparison to this experience, with a part of me still not trusting. I felt as if I were still dreaming, in a fairyland in the woods, my faceless monster having been transformed into a tender, gentle giant.

The next four days included his washing and combing my hair, showing me his land, massaging my back, nights of lying in front of the fireplace. I felt I had been transported from my nightmare existence to this amazing experience. We lay on a bearskin rug in front of the fireplace and Joseph vividly expressed his dreams, his plans for our future. After all else and an established feeling of trust, his lovemaking was as gentle as any love I had ever created in my girlish fantasies.

I came back into my body from the regression knowing the man spirit desired me to marry was a previous incarnation of Joseph and that I would be safe to marry him. What I didn't know, but would later learn after only nine months of marriage, was that my husband, even though he had been involved with spiritual studies for fifteen years, found it impossible to be married to someone who was psychic. I railed at my soul after this experience, feeling deceived and used. The soul explained that in each life we have Freewill and that my husband's freewill had to be considered, even though the soul would have chosen for the relationship to be otherwise. Through the years, many relationships were brought to me, some just suggested and some lived through for various reasons, many of which were karmic.

At this time in history, since we are moving from the Piscean Age into the Aquarian Age, it is necessary to experience many different kinds of relationships. The traditional one, marriage, or one romantic relationship per life, is rare. We are finishing many thousands of years of karma in this one lifetime. Karma will no longer be carried over from one lifetime to the next in the Aquarian Age. We are on the fast track of evolution, between Ages, between planes and between the old and new version of the Human species. Time has sped up by the tightening of the Ring-Pass-Not; therefore, life is complex, and much more will need to be accomplished, of necessity, during these lives we are now living.

Many people have asked for more explanation of the Oversoul. Not many people have written about this concept other than Seth through Jane Roberts in her *Oversoul Seven* series, which I highly recommend to you. I've also found some mentions of the Oversoul in Ralph Waldo Emerson's work and the Alice Bailey Blue Books channeled from the Master Djwhal Khul.

I came to know of the concept of the Oversoul from my own soul communication. Early on in my direct communication with Spirit, because I came from a Christian religious background, my knowledge of the Universe, Spirit, the Spiritual Hierarchy, Evolution, Reincarnation, The Intergalactic Federation and the Oversoul were nonexistent. Spirit has been gentle in expanding my conscious awareness once the first door between my conscious mind and Spirit was flung open in 1982.

I was totally blown away by what I saw and experienced in the regressions I experienced with the psychologist. It was impossible from that time on for me not to believe in past lives. I was then given a method by my soul of how to safely regress other people.

I did regressions of others for several years. I would put the person in a relaxed state and then guide them into the life their soul suggested to me through telepathic contact with their soul. When they began to perceive either images or awarenesses, I would follow along with them as they viewed the life to make sure they didn't get caught up in the story and begin to make it up. At the end of the session, we would energetically clear the karma of the life, heal their cellular memory of the life and deliberately bring forward any talents or love they had in that life into the present life.

Sometimes people came back for more than one session. The first time I regressed a person and they showed up in a life that was during the exact time we had seen them in another life, I became very suspicious and unsure of the method. I challenged my soul for an explanation. It was explained that we carry the cellular memory of the lives that have been lived by everyone in our Oversoul. Because of this, it is possible for many people to believe they have been some famous person, such as Abraham Lincoln, George Washington, Joan of Arc, or a certain Pharaoh, etc. Once an entity has acquired a large consciousness and they transcend, they are then free to split their consciousness and project many aspects of their consciousness back to Earth for expanded experience. Because of this, we may have many other members of our same Oversoul on the planet at one time. These parts are spiritually referred to as "aspects" of one Oversoul, or kindred spirits. Some people refer to them as soul mates. It is also why we cannot tell a person how many lives they have lived.

It is not unusual to meet someone else from your same Oversoul. When this happens, there is usually a sense of familiarity with that person. This does not necessarily mean the encounter will feel positive. It is usually very highly charged energetically. If we meet another person from our Oversoul who is a member of the opposite sex and of the same approximate age, the energy is often so strong that we assume the encounter is for the purpose of a romantic relationship, and many people jump into bed before they have any real spiritual understanding of what the soul had in mind for the relationship. It is not uncommon for the Oversoul to bring together two or more members of one Oversoul when one or more of the members are going through a traumatic or challenging change in their lives. It is also not unusual if the Oversoul has in mind a large project it wishes to accomplish through the aspects, which would require multiple persons or talents to complete the project.

# 9.

# Soul Retrieval
# Mending The Fragmented Self

There are non-ordinary realities parallel to our own. We can learn through meditation to enter these dimensions or realities. It is possible for parts of our essential life-energy to split off and become lost in one of these "non-ordinary realities" or other dimensions due to trauma.

Soul loss happens whenever we experience trauma. The word "soul" has taken on many meanings. The soul is defined in the dictionary as "The principle of life, commonly regarded as an entity distinct from the body; the spiritual parts in contrast to the purely physical." According to the dictionary, our language also regards the soul as the seat of emotions, feelings, or sentiments.

Here we will use the term to simply mean our vital essence. A part of our vital essence separates from the body in order to survive the experience of trauma by escaping the full impact of the pain of trauma. What constitutes trauma varies from one individual to another. Soul loss can be caused by whatever a person experiences as traumatic, even if another person would not experience it as such. We often find soul loss as a result of such traumas as incest, abuse, loss of a loved one, loss of a job, loss of a home, experiencing an earthquake, tsunami or tornado, surgery, accident, illness, miscarriage, abortion, the vanishing-twin syndrome, the stress of combat, torture, addiction, rape, witnessing a murder, or abandonment.

The vanishing twin syndrome occurs when, at the beginning of a pregnancy, two embryos are forming and the mother's body will not support the creation of two bodies. When one of the soul aspects pulls back and decides not to come into incarnation at that time, the physical matter of one embryo is absorbed into the mother's body or into the body of the surviving embryo. The twin that continues to form feels the loss of the being they expected to join them in the incarnation. The feelings are similar to the feelings of soul loss.

People who have experienced soul loss or the vanishing-twin syndrome often experience feelings of incompleteness, disconnection or feelings of abandonment.

Although the term "soul loss" may be unfamiliar to you, examples of it are well known under other names. A beloved spouse, child, or friend dies, and the survivor also "deadens" for a while. We feel as if the light has gone from our existence, as if we are sleepwalking or there is a cloud or blanket between us and everyone else. Or we return from having major surgery and do not feel as if we have come fully out of the anesthesia, or we no longer feel like our same self. After being involved in an automobile accident, we can feel "spaced out." It is my witnessing experience that when we sustain a violent blow to our physical and etheric body, our energy field actually shifts at least twelve inches to the left. This is what can possibly cause the body to go into shock and to experience feelings of disassociation.

A person involved in an abusive intimate relationship may be aware of being locked into destructive patterns but feel too weak and powerless to move away. Or in leaving the relationship, he or she might feel as though a part of them was left behind with the partner.

A part of the soul energy may leave a child who is abused, does not feel loved, or who feels abandoned by his or her parents, or by being continually exposed to parents who fight and yell. A fall from a bicycle, a building, or a wall can cause a person to experience shock or separation from their etheric body. One sign of soul loss is a gap in childhood memory. Persons experiencing soul loss frequently say they feel fragmented in some way, or an essential part of their selves is missing. If the trauma is severe enough, the person can become dissociated. Dissociation is the separation of whole segments of the personality from the mainstream of consciousness, and can result in feelings of estrangement or depersonalization. Chronic depression can be another symptom of soul loss. Coma is an extreme example of soul loss.

In some way, most of us experience some degree of soul loss. Some people have been more deeply traumatized by life; they may seem quite "dispirited." Life has been kinder to others; they may not have needed to protect themselves so completely. Regardless of the degree of trauma, however, most people I know yearn for a fuller sense of vitality and connectedness to life.

The trauma of adolescence and puberty can cause a person to disassociate. Often, an adolescent will involve themselves in sexual activity at a very young age to attempt to fit in. When this happens before the emotional body is developed to handle such events, parts of the personality will shut down and parts of the soul essence are separated.

When individuals find their lives too difficult to endure, such a large part of the soul retreats that the body is more or less run from a distance. These people live spaced out, no longer in the body, having a continual out-of-body experience. The use of drugs can first assist them to move out of the body, and they then find the state so much easier to bear that they remain out of their body. Extended periods of out-of-body experience can leave a person with the feeling that their life is not worth living. They have lost the feeling of being fully alive and connected to their body. Most people using drugs and excessive alcohol are attempting to acquire this state and to remain there.

In the shamanic culture, all things are thought to be permeated by Spirit. Every earthly form is animated with its own soul or life force. The well-being of any particular life form is dependent on its spiritual harmony with other forms. Imbalances or displacement in the spiritual essence of a living being can cause debilitation and disease. For shamans the World over, illness has always been seen as a spiritual predicament.

According to the shaman Sandra Ingerman, the word "shaman", originating from the Tungus tribe of Siberia, means "one who sees in the dark." The shaman uses the ability to see "with the strong eye" or "with the heart" to travel to hidden spirit worlds to find information and to perform acts that will heal an ailing individual or community. If you wish to learn more about the shamanic form of soul retrieval, you may be interested in reading *Soul Retrieval* by Sandra Ingerman.

In addition to soul theft or rape of the soul, some shamanic cultures relate soul loss to interference by ghosts as well as by other Human beings. In South America, according to books I've read and shamans I've spoken with, shamans in both the Andes and the Amazon believe the soul can either stray away under frightening conditions or be abducted by a Spirit or a ghost.

Leaving our energy fields open, failing to stay grounded, using drugs and excessive alcohol leaves our energy field open to invasion by other energies. At this time, Earth and Humanity are in the middle of the Fourth dimension with all the souls who have died and not made it into the Fifth dimension. Christians would have identified the dimension we are now living in as hell and the Fifth dimension and higher as heaven. Living in a dimension where there are so many bodiless souls wandering around leaves us open to occasional if not permanent possession by one or more of these lost souls. It is extremely important to give up operating empathically, to ground ourselves and to create zones of energy around our body that are our protection from intrusion by other souls.

When a person dies who is addicted to a substance such as nicotine, drugs, alcohol, sex, overeating, the urge to dominate or rape, anger, gambling, or the misuse of power, their etheric body moves into the Fourth dimension. These addictions cause them to have low levels of energy that make it impossible for them to move through the energetic barrier that holds the negative thought forms of Humans close to the Earth to keep us from contaminating the rest of the Universe. They are in what Christians would think of as hell because they still have the addiction without a body through which to experience relief; therefore, they will attach themselves to a body using their drug or behavior of choice.

It is possible for us to assist stuck souls to move on to a higher dimension by calling on the Archangel Michael and the Band of Mercy to escort a lost soul into the light. Never get into a confrontation with a lost or invading spirit. Always call upon this Band of Mercy Angels to dispossess or escort lost souls.

At this time in history, overcoming being empathic in favor of being consciously multidimensional is extremely important for our mental, physical and emotional health. Walking around in hell as an emotional sponge is tantamount to suicide.

Many people, when first reading it, think the grounding and connecting process sounds too easy and doubt that it will work. Trust me. I was so empathic after giving up Valium that I could not even go into a grocery store to shop and get all the way to the back of the store to get milk without being overcome with anxiety from the thought forms other people were carrying. We did not become empathic overnight. We developed being empathic in the crib in order to get our needs met and to be safe. It is a deeply ingrained habit. It is actually against Spiritual Law to merge into another person's emotional and energy body.

There is a safer, saner, better way to live as a consciously multi-dimensional person. You may need to do the grounding and connecting process several times a day at first until you have trained yourself not to merge with other people energetically and emotionally. You will then be able to connect to other people from your Oversoul to theirs, which will make your communication with others clearer and stronger. You will also be gifted from their Oversoul with any information that is appropriate for you to know.

Working with another person, such as a therapist, in meditation, it is possible to move into other realities to retrieve the lost parts of our souls. It is also possible to meet and converse and receive inspiration and wisdom from higher levels of ourselves. It is time for us to become all we are capable of being. In order to do this, we must learn spiritual protection as well as realizing where we are dimensionally and energetically. It is time to learn Interdimensional travel to meet all the parts of our Oversouls.

I highly recommend you communicate only with the highest level of your Oversoul and create a rapport with that level of your Oversoul. I recommend you appoint this level of your soul to be your gatekeeper or receptionist between you and the Spirit World and all other dimensions. In the dimension in which we are now living, because it contains so many lost souls, it is important to be clear that any information you are receiving is only from the highest level of your own soul. Many lost souls would love to connect, use, effect and speak in this dimension through live bodies. Maintaining a censor within your own soul energy can be very reassuring. This level of yourself, when given the assignment through your intention, can relay to you only those things spiritually that are yours to know, and keep away from you any potentially interfering or possessing entities that would love to use your body. This level of you can assist you to locate and reconnect any lost parts of your life essence.

# 10.

# Walk-Ins – Walk-Outs – Soul Transfers – Soul Braiding – Soul Merging – Composites

In 1982, while meditating, I received a message from my soul. It was one of many messages I began to receive after learning to meditate. I meditated and wrote the information that came into my mind. It was suggested that I read Ruth Montgomery's books. I went to a bookstore and found that indeed such an author did exist. I bought all the books and read them in the order in which she had written them. I was fascinated and relieved to learn that she had received the information for the books in the same way I had received the suggestion to read her books. I had never heard of anyone else who communicated spiritually in this way. I felt relief. I, at last, had proof I was not alone and I was not crazy.

My ex-husband attempted to have me committed because I was leaving him, and because I had changed so much. He would often say, "You're no longer the person I married." We went to a psychologist, chosen by my husband, for what I thought was marriage counseling. At the end of the session I was asked by the counselor, "What is the worst-case scenario you can possibly imagine happening if you go through with your plan to take your children, move to Oklahoma and marry this priest?" I thought for a few moments and said, "He could abandon me, I could be left with no home, no spouse to support me, no job, and I would have to allow my children to come back to Texas to live with their Dad. I could be left totally alone."

"Could you survive that?" asked the psychologist.

"Yes, I could, but I certainly don't expect to have to. I trust this man I'm going to marry with my life," I replied defiantly.

The psychologist then turned to my husband and said, "Mr. King, I would have to say she is the sanest person who has ever entered my office, because she knows exactly what she desires and she is willing to live with the consequences of her choices no matter the outcome."

I realized in his addressing my husband, and not me, the purpose of our meeting was not for marriage counseling. The next day, when I met with an attorney about the divorce, he informed me, that by Texas law, a husband could have his wife committed if he could find three psychologists who would attest to her mental instability. I became painfully and fearfully aware that I had been at a sanity hearing, not a marriage counseling session.

One of the later books in the Montgomery series is *Strangers Among Us*. It was published in New York by Fawcett Crest in 1979, the year I moved from Texas. While I was reading page 11-12, an unusual thing happened. My body began to vibrate and I began to weep for no obvious reason. Through my tears I read the following:

"Enlightened beings, who, after successfully completing numerous incarnations, having attained sufficient awareness of the meaning of life can forego the time-consuming process of birth and childhood, returning directly to adult bodies.

"A Walk-in is a high-minded entity who is permitted to take over the body of another Human being who wishes to depart. Since a Walk-in must never enter a body without the permission of its owner this is not to be confused with those well-publicized cases (Such as were described in The Three Faces of Eve, the Exorcist, et al.) in which multiple egos or evil Spirits are vying for possession of an inhabited body.

"The motivation for a Walk-in is Humanitarian. A walk-in returns as a physical Human in order to help others help themselves, planting seed-concepts that will grow and flourish for the benefit of Humankind.

"Some of the World's greatest spiritual and political leaders, scientists, and philosophers in ages past are said to have been Walk-ins, but during these final decades of the twentieth century the pace has been steadily accelerating, and many more of them are entering mature physical bodies to prepare us for the energetic shift that the Earth will experience as it moves vibrationally into the Fifth dimension.

"Not all Walk-ins are towering leaders. Many are working quietly among us today, going about their unsung task of helping us to understand ourselves, to seek inner guidance, and to develop a philosophy that will sustain us through the trying times ahead.

"You may know a Walk-in in your own office, or in your community. They seldom reveal themselves, because to do so could imperil the good work for which they returned to be a physical Human.

"In fact, you yourself may be a Walk-in! (An electrical current hit my body and jolted me.) Since the memory pattern of the departing entity survives intact, Walk-ins are sometimes unaware of their altered status for several years after the substitution has been effected."

I slowly lowered the book to my lap and sat staring into space. My inner voice said quite clearly, "You are a Walk-in. You joined this body in 1969 during the pregnancy of your first child. You have completed the first entity's karmic contract. It is time to allow the original entity freedom to return to the soul. It is time for you to be the sole occupant in the body. It is time for you to begin accomplishing the larger planetary contract now assigned to this body."

"I don't believe this. What are you talking about? This is the most bizarre thing I've ever heard. I've never heard of such a thing. I don't believe this can happen to a person. You've got to be wrong about this. I know I've changed, but lots of people change. That doesn't mean I'm not the same person," I raged at my soul.

But at some level I was intrigued. If, in fact, such a thing could happen and had indeed happened to me, it would explain so many things. It would explain the confusion of the past thirteen years. It would explain the inner conflict. At that time, I had felt as if I were living in a cocoon, waiting and somehow expecting to become something else. I kept feeling as if there were somehow more of me than I knew or understood. I identified, for the first time in my life, with the symbol of the butterfly. I began to collect butterflies. I was desperately seeking something, but I didn't understand what I was searching for. I felt the church had somehow something to do with what I was looking for, so I spent as much time as possible working at the church and attending services. I volunteered for everything.

But, if what the author, and seemingly my soul, was suggesting were true, it would explain my ability to suddenly be able to quit taking the Valium. It would explain my ability to have the strength to leave my husband and children, my home, my security, my extended family, my community responsibilities, despite my intense inner conflict about those choices. It would explain my burning desire to know the Truth, to understand God, and the Universe. It would explain why, even though the option was offered, I could not return to Texas to rejoin my ex-husband, my children, and my previous life after my fiancé's death. It would explain why the soul had used this method to get me out of my life in Texas and left me alone in Oklahoma. It would explain why, for the first time in my life, I cut my hair into a pixie cut and became a blonde, when all my life I had worn my hair long and never dyed it. It would explain my sudden desire to pierce my ears and to stop wearing nail polish. It would explain my desire to dress in a more colorful, relaxed and less tailored fashion. It would explain my sudden impulse to travel, to paint, to write, to be a vegetarian, to exercise, to dance, to read and meditate to seek answers, beyond those in the *Bible*. It would explain so many things.

But how could this have happened and I not be aware of it? If this had happened, how could I still remember so many things so clearly and other things about my life (or was it now our life?) How could my memories be so foggy, or in some cases, have no memory at all? Why did I not remember where I came from to join this body? Why did I not remember who I was before and what I was doing before agreeing to come here? Why did I not remember why I was here? These questions puzzled me deeply, in light of this new information. I had no one to talk with except my soul. I tried, but was unsuccessful, in communicating with Ruth Montgomery through her publisher.

I picked the book up again and began to read further. The writer explained that the memories are in the cells of the bodies. She explained that the Walk-in would have access to these memories. Under normal circumstances, the new entity would cohabitate in the body to familiarize themselves with the movements, beliefs, habits, family, and routine of the original entity. She explained that, in order to qualify to take over a body, an entity must agree to complete the karmic contract of the original soul. Only then would they be free to use the body for their own mission or contract. My soul explained that, at the time of my move to Oklahoma, I had not completed the karmic contract of the original entity.

In questioning my soul further, it was explained that it was not advantageous, nor thought wise by the soul, to allow the Walk-in to immediately remember where they came from or their reason for taking over the body. Their larger mission or purpose for coming to Earth would have a tendency to seem too big or too overwhelming to a new Walk-in. It was necessary and more important for integration into the body that the karmic life of the host be completed first. It was felt, by the soul, that to remember these things immediately would be even more confusing and would complicate the integration of the new soul "aspect" with the body. This was the first time I had heard the terminology "aspect" in reference to the soul. I questioned this terminology. It was explained to me that the soul aspects are grouped into families of souls called an Oversoul, very much like a spiritual family tree, as in genealogy. It was suggested that I energetically observe the silver cord above a person's head, the silver cord and to follow that cord with my inner vision. When I tried this, I observed that the cord continued beyond this dimension and extended into a place where it connected to other energies. I observed, as I entered into each dimension, that more than one energy was sometimes connected within a given dimension. As I continued to follow the cord, I saw these points of light, or beings, soul aspects, as my soul was now referencing to them, were all energetically connected. My soul explained that each soul aspect is a part of a much larger soul energy family. Ultimately, at a higher level, each of these Oversouls is connected, and beyond that, all souls are sourced from the Creator God, the Creator of All Universes. All living things are created by, and are a part of, the One God.

It was explained that each aspect, prior to incarnating, creates a soul contract stating what they wish to attempt or accomplish in any given lifetime. These contracts reflect what the Oversoul desires to experience, to learn, to accomplish, and to balance karmically for the entire Oversoul. Often, groups of aspects from one Oversoul will incarnate during the same time frame to assist each other, or to accomplish a group mission. It was revealed that, in the cells of our bodies, we not only store the memories of this life, but the memories of all the lives of all the members of our Oversoul. My guidance relayed that it was similar to an enormous video library in the DNA. It was explained that this is why several people, who might be regressed to see their past lives, might all believe they had been some famous figure in history. They would all be right, even though this does not compute to our linear, left-brain, logical thinking, or our concept of linear time. All members of one Oversoul would hold the composite memory of each incarnation. It was further explained that we are all jointly responsible for balancing the karma created by our Oversoul family. I wondered as I heard this, "Is this relational to the 'sins of the father being passed down for generations', as mentioned in the *Bible*?" It was explained that a person might agree to come to Earth to balance karma for the Oversoul that they had not personally, physically participated in creating in a previous life. But through a desire to serve the soul family, they would take on such a responsibility.

It was further suggested by my sou, for me to read Ruth Montgomery's *Aliens Among Us*, which was even more "far out" in my opinion at the time.

At that time, I had no belief or experience with extra-terrestrials

I also read *Threshold to Tomorrow* by Ruth Montgomery, in which she interviewed some known Walk-ins. In this volume, she tells about the present lives and accomplishments of several Walk-ins. I noticed, in her book, that one of the Walk-ins lived in Oklahoma. She had just published a book of her own Walk-in experience. I ordered the book and eagerly read her story. Her book, *Messengers of Hope*, by Carol W. Parrish-Harra, is available from The Village Bookstore, P. O. Box 1274, Tahlequah, OK 74465.

I related in many ways to Carol's story. There were similarities in our backgrounds. She had been a banker. She had been married to a firefighter. She was a mother. She was now living in Oklahoma. I went to visit her and her community near Tahlequah, OK. I was impressed by her knowledge and by what had been created through her and her husband. But when I met her, I could not connect to her personality. I suffered another extreme disappointment. I was hoping to find someone I could talk with about my experience, someone with whom I could relate. I felt even more alone and confused. I continued to communicate with my soul, which was why I was not finding people with whom I could communicate Third-dimensionally. It forced me to communicate more directly with my soul. I later learned, during this period of my development, that perfecting my ability to communicate with my soul and developing soul trust was mandatory to my future growth.

Once I became more used to the idea of being a Walk-in, and the original aspect successfully returned to the soul, I found no real need to mention to anyone that I was a Walk-in. It is, in my opinion, not relevant. We are all here with missions. The important thing is to get on with our missions, not so much to dwell on whom we were before, where we came from, or how we got here. My only reason for writing this information and including it is for the purpose of clarification for other Walk-ins, and to explain the concept in more detail.

It is my understanding from Spirit that once a person makes the decision they no longer want to live, whether they deliberately attempt to take their life or not, they become a candidate to become a Walk-in. A Walk-in never happens without the consent, at the soul level, of both aspects of the Oversoul. The aspect, which is depressed or desires to leave the life, is observed by the Oversoul. In the beginning of the process, a higher vibrational aspect will over light the body in order for the entity to have more energy with which to accomplish the original contract. This additional energy sometimes will make it possible for them to restore their desire to deal with the life circumstances which previously seemed overwhelming, conflicting or insurmountable. If this additional energy does not help the entity to cope, does not "rescue" them from their desire to leave, additional measures are then taken. Often times, this temporary over lighting solves the depression and strengthens the person's will to continue in the life. When the Oversoul feels the aspect is stable, the additional energy is withdrawn and the life continues according to the original plan. If, however, the original aspect does not stabilize, the second energy stays and plans are made at the level of the Oversoul for either a "soul merger", "soul braiding" or "soul exchange" Walk-in to take place. Ultimately a decision may be made to use the body as a "composite".

Each case is different. When a "soul merger" occurs, both aspects of the Oversoul remain in the body. The original personality agrees to sublimate to the higher vibrational energy aspect that has come to over light, rescue the body. The incoming entity becomes the dominant force in the body. The first aspect does not leave the body. They agree to merge their resources and continue the karmic contract. The first entity stays to assist with the larger contract, which has been agreed to at the level of the Oversoul by the Walk-in. In these cases, the souls braid their consciousness together. There is no Walk-out.

In the case of the "soul exchange," the Walk-in, the rescuing soul aspect, always comes from the same Oversoul and there is always a Walk-out when the original soul aspect returns to the Oversoul for reassignment.

In the case of "soul merger" and "soul braiding," there is no "Walk-out". Occasionally, after a Walk-in has successfully merged with a body and integrated, and the first aspect has successfully returned to the Oversoul, further decisions will be made at the level of the Oversoul with the soul aspect in the body. One of the possible decisions is for additional aspects from the Oversoul to occasionally over light the body to teach, to write, to perform or to accomplish artwork or inventions. In other situations, it is agreed that several entities will combine their energies to integrate into the Walk-in body to accomplish a larger mission, planned by the Spiritual Hierarchy. When a Walk-in agrees to be used by the Spiritual Hierarchy as a "composite," additional aspects merge with the body over a longer period of time. Each merger usually takes from six months to a year. Each aspect relinquishes its personality and merges only its energy, consciousness and talents into the host body. The body is then capable of being utilized by a "group mind". A "group mind" is a group of beings, within the Spiritual Hierarchy, who have an interest in one chosen field of expertise. An assigned Ascended Master from the Spiritual Hierarchy sponsors the body with energy and knowledge. An Ascended Master is a being that has advanced spiritually to the point they are no longer required to reincarnate into a physical body. They serve Humanity from a higher dimension, influencing energetically, telepathically and intuitively the events taking place on Earth with Humanity's permission. Because of the Universal Laws of Free Will and Non-Interference, one level of life, or species, is not allowed by spiritual law to intervene in the evolution of another level of life or species without permission from a member of that species. More and more Walk-ins, in my experience, are agreeing to become composite vehicles. This allows externalization of the Spiritual Hierarchy to assist in the evolution of Earth and Humanity.

After many years of serving as a channel for the Hierarchy and members of the Federation, I agreed to become a composite. Periodically, through the years, I have undergone additional soul over lightings and soul merges.

In later years, I met another woman named Juelle who published her story in a book entitled *The Walk-in*, which is available from Book Partners, Inc, P. O. Box 922, Wilsonville, Oregon 97070. I met a therapist who wrote a book called *From Sirius to Earth: A Therapist Discovers A Soul Exchange* by Evelyn Fuqua, Ph.D., available through Oughten House Publishers, 1-888-673-3748. I have not read the series of books written in the 1960's by Lobsang Rampa, but I understand they include information about the concept of Walk-ins. A woman named Liz Nelson contacted me several years after I became aware I was a Walk-in. Liz, through Spirit's suggestion, started an organization called Walk-ins for Evolution, WE International. Liz arranged conferences for walk-ins and those interested in the subject for years, but Liz has since left the planet so the organization no longer exists.

**If you feel you are a Walk-in, know someone who is, or wish to meet other Walk-Ins, you may go on the Internet and do a search on the word "Walk-in".**

***Bless you on your journey of self-discovery.***

## Other Books by bj King

*Pentimento: Diary of a Walk-In*

*Self-Mastery Of Mind And Emotion*

*Who Are You And What On Earth Are You*

*Life After Life*

*Old Loves Are Seldom Finished ... When New Loves Begin*

*I Am Presence and Violet Flame*

*The Universal Laws and Jesus' Meaning of The Beatitudes*

*Manual for Spiritual Maturity*

*The Master Jesus Speaks*

*Life is A Spiritual Game*

*Principles of Truth*

www.ingramcontent.com/pod-product-compliance
Lightning Source LLC
Chambersburg PA
CBHW020356170426
43200CB00005B/190